About the Author

Valda Hilley is a computer consultant and author who has written computer books on all the familiar versions of Windows, as well as numerous articles filled with technobabble and secret information. She demystifies and decodes the mysteries of Windows 2000 Professional for the rest of the world in *Windows 2000 Professional For Dummies Quick Reference.*

ABOUT IDG BOOKS WORLDWIDE

Welcome to the world of IDG Books Worldwide.

IDG Books Worldwide, Inc., is a subsidiary of International Data Group, the world's largest publisher of computer-related information and the leading global provider of information services on information technology. IDG was founded more than 30 years ago by Patrick J. McGovern and now employs more than 9,000 people worldwide. IDG publishes more than 290 computer publications in over 75 countries. More than 90 million people read one or more IDG publications each month.

Launched in 1990, IDG Books Worldwide is today the #1 publisher of best-selling computer books in the United States. We are proud to have received eight awards from the Computer Press Association in recognition of editorial excellence and three from Computer Currents' First Annual Readers' Choice Awards. Our best-selling ...For Dummies® series has more than 50 million copies in print with translations in 31 languages. IDG Books Worldwide, through a joint venture with IDG's Hi-Tech Beijing, became the first U.S. publisher to publish a computer book in the People's Republic of China. In record time, IDG Books Worldwide has become the first choice for millions of readers around the world who want to learn how to better manage their businesses.

Our mission is simple: Every one of our books is designed to bring extra value and skill-building instructions to the reader. Our books are written by experts who understand and care about our readers. The knowledge base of our editorial staff comes from years of experience in publishing, education, and journalism — experience we use to produce books to carry us into the new millennium. In short, we care about books, so we attract the best people. We devote special attention to details such as audience, interior design, use of icons, and illustrations. And because we use an efficient process of authoring, editing, and desktop publishing our books electronically, we can spend more time ensuring superior content and less time on the technicalities of making books.

You can count on our commitment to deliver high-quality books at competitive prices on topics you want to read about. At IDG Books Worldwide, we continue in the IDG tradition of delivering quality for more than 30 years. You'll find no better book on a subject than one from IDG Books Worldwide.

IDG BOOKS WORLDWIDE

John Kilcullen
Chairman and CEO
IDG Books Worldwide, Inc.

Steven Berkowitz
President and Publisher
IDG Books Worldwide, Inc.

VIII WINNER

Eighth Annual Computer Press Awards ≥1992

IX WINNER

Ninth Annual Computer Press Awards ≥1993

X WINNER

Tenth Annual Computer Press Awards ≥1994

XI WINNER

Eleventh Annual Computer Press Awards ≥1995

IDG is the world's leading IT media, research and exposition company. Founded in 1964, IDG had 1997 revenues of $2.05 billion and has more than 9,000 employees worldwide. IDG offers the widest range of media options that reach IT buyers in 75 countries representing 95% of worldwide IT spending. IDG's diverse product and services portfolio spans six key areas including print publishing, online publishing, expositions and conferences, market research, education and training, and global marketing services. More than 90 million people read one or more of IDG's 290 magazines and newspapers, including IDG's leading global brands — Computerworld, PC World, Network World, Macworld and the Channel World family of publications. IDG Books Worldwide is one of the fastest-growing computer book publishers in the world, with more than 700 titles in 36 languages. The "...For Dummies®" series alone has more than 50 million copies in print. IDG offers online users the largest network of technology-specific Web sites around the world through IDG.net (http://www.idg.net), which comprises more than 225 targeted Web sites in 55 countries worldwide. International Data Corporation (IDC) is the world's largest provider of information technology data, analysis and consulting, with research centers in over 41 countries and more than 400 research analysts worldwide. IDG World Expo is a leading producer of more than 168 globally branded conferences and expositions in 35 countries including E3 (Electronic Entertainment Expo), Macworld Expo, ComNet, Windows World Expo, ICE (Internet Commerce Expo), Agenda, DEMO, and Spotlight. IDG's training subsidiary, ExecuTrain, is the world's largest computer training company, with more than 230 locations worldwide and 785 training courses. IDG Marketing Services helps industry-leading IT companies build international brand recognition by developing global integrated marketing programs via IDG's print, online and exposition products worldwide. Further information about the company can be found at www.idg.com.   1/24/99

Publisher's Acknowledgments

We're proud of this book; please register your comments through our IDG Books Worldwide Online Registration Form located at http://my2cents.dummies.com.

Some of the people who helped bring this book to market include the following:

Acquisitions, Editorial, and Media Development

Project Editor: Pat O'Brien

Acquisitions Editor: David Mayhew

Copy Editors: Ted Cains, Barry Childs-Helton, Stephanie Koutek

Technical Editor: Bob Correll

Editorial Manager: Rev Mengle

Editorial Assistant: Jamila Pree

Production

Project Coordinator: Regina Snyder

Layout and Graphics: Angela F. Hunckler, Barry Offringa, Brent Savage, Jacque Schneider, Brian Torwelle, Dan Whetstine

Proofreaders: Laura Albert, John Greenough, Henry Lazarek, Marianne Santy, Rebecca Senninger

Indexer: Sherry Massey

General and Administrative

IDG Books Worldwide, Inc.: John Kilcullen, CEO; Steven Berkowitz, President and Publisher

IDG Books Technology Publishing Group: Richard Swadley, Senior Vice President and Publisher; Walter Bruce III, Vice President and Associate Publisher; Joseph Wikert, Associate Publisher; Mary Bednarek, Branded Product Development Director; Mary Corder, Editorial Director; Barry Pruett, Publishing Manager; Michelle Baxter, Publishing Manager

IDG Books Consumer Publishing Group: Roland Elgey, Senior Vice President and Publisher; Kathleen A. Welton, Vice President and Publisher; Kevin Thornton, Acquisitions Manager; Kristin A. Cocks, Editorial Director

IDG Books Internet Publishing Group: Brenda McLaughlin, Senior Vice President and Publisher; Diane Graves Steele, Vice President and Associate Publisher; Sofia Marchant, Online Marketing Manager

IDG Books Production for Dummies Press: Debbie Stailey, Associate Director of Production; Cindy L. Phipps, Manager of Project Coordination, Production Proofreading, and Indexing; Tony Augsburger, Manager of Prepress, Reprints, and Systems; Laura Carpenter, Production Control Manager; Shelley Lea, Supervisor of Graphics and Design; Debbie J. Gates, Production Systems Specialist; Robert Springer, Supervisor of Proofreading; Kathie Schutte, Production Supervisor

Dummies Packaging and Book Design: Patty Page, Manager, Promotions Marketing

♦

The publisher would like to give special thanks to Patrick J. McGovern, without whom this book would not have been possible.

♦

Contents at a Glance

Introduction 1

How to Use This Book 1

Intro I: Getting to Know Windows 2000 5

Part II: Working with Files and Folders 23

Part III: Working with Programs 45

Part IV: Using All Those Accessories 55

Part V: Working the Web with Internet Explorer 5 77

Part VI: Using Outlook Express E-Mail and News 89

Part VII: Print(ing) or Perish 105

Part VIII: Networking Near and Far 119

Part IX: Personalizing Your Computer 143

Glossary: Techie Talk 157

Index 163

Book Registration Information ....Back of Book

Table of Contents

Introduction: How to Use This Book 1

How This Book Is Organized 2
    Part I: Getting to Know Windows 2000 2
    Part II: Working with Files and Folders 2
    Part III: Working with Programs 2
    Part IV: Using All Those Accessories 2
    Part V: Working the Web with Internet Explorer 5 2
    Part VI: Using Outlook Express E-Mail and News 2
    Part VII: Print(ing) or Perish 3
    Part VIII: Networking Near and Far 3
    Part IX: Personalizing Your Computer 3
    Glossary: Techie Talk 3
    The Cast of Icons 3

Part I: Getting to Know Windows 2000 5

Desktop 6
Dialog Boxes 7
    Closing a dialog box 8
    Making selections 8
Help! 9
    Finding a topic in Help 10
    Getting information on dialog box settings 10
    Printing a Help topic 11
    Searching for Help with Search 11
    Starting Help 12
    Using the Help Contents 12
Mousing Around 13
    Clicking 13
    Double-clicking 13
    Dragging 13
    Right-clicking 13
Selecting Items 14
    Selecting disks 14
    Selecting files 14
    Selecting folders 14
Shutting Down Windows 2000 Professional 14
Start Menu 15
Starting Windows 2000 Professional 16
Window Parts 16
    Control-menu commands 17
    Menus 18
    Scroll bars 19
    Shortcut menus 19
    Title bars 20

Toolbars 20
Window buttons 21

Part II: Working with Files and Folders 23

Associating File Types 24
Changing a File or Folder Name 24
Changing the Recycle Bin's Size 25
Copying a File to a Disk 26
Copying Files or Folders 27
    Using the mouse to drag and drop a copy 27
    Using the menu to copy a file or folder 28
Creating Folders 29
Deleting a File or Folder 30
Emptying the Recycle Bin 31
Finding a File or Folder 32
Moving Files or Folders 34
    Using the mouse 34
    Using menu commands 34
My Documents Folder 35
Opening a File 36
Recycle Bin 36
Removing Files Permanently When You Delete Them ˙ 36
Retrieving Deleted Files or Shortcuts 37
Sending Files to Other Places 38
Sorting Files 39
Viewing a File's Properties 40
Viewing Files 41
Viewing Graphics Files 42
Windows Explorer 42

Part III: Working with Programs 45

Adding a Shortcut on the Desktop 46
Adding Programs to the Start Menu or Programs Menu 47
Adding Programs to Your System 48
Clearing Documents from the Documents Menu 49
Quitting an MS-DOS Program 49
Quitting Programs 49
Removing Program Shortcuts from the Start Menu 50
Removing Programs from Your System 51
Starting an MS-DOS Program 52
Starting Programs by Using the Run Command 52
Starting Programs by Using the Start Button 53
Starting Programs Each Time Windows 2000 Starts 53
Switching between Programs 54

Part IV: Using All Those Accessories 55

About the Accessories 56
Calculator 57
    Quick basic math with Calculator 58
    Scientific number-crunching with Calculator 59
CD Player 60
Character Map 61
Games You Can Play 62
HyperTerminal 63
    Starting HyperTerminal 63
    Setting up a new connection 63
    Calling a remote computer 64
    Sending a file to a remote computer 64
    Receiving a file from a remote computer 64
    Changing port settings 65
    Saving a HyperTerminal session 65
Media Player 66
    Starting Media Player 66
    Opening and Playing a Media File 66
Notepad 67
    Starting Notepad 67
    Keeping a log 67
Paint 68
    Starting Paint 68
    Opening a file 68
    Using a picture as the desktop background 69
    Printing a picture 69
    Setting margins and changing orientation 69
Sound Recorder 69
    Starting Sound Recorder 69
    Opening and playing a sound file 70
    Recording and saving a sound 70
    Altering a sound file 70
Volume Control 71
    Starting Volume Control 71
    Adjusting playback volume 72
    Adjusting recording volume 72
    Adjusting voice-input volume 72
WordPad 72
    Starting WordPad 73
    Creating a new document 73
    Saving changes 73
    Opening a document 73
    Undoing an action 74
    Deleting text 74

Selecting text 74
Searching for text 74
Inserting date and time 74
Changing text wrap 75
Inserting bullets 75
Changing fonts 75
Previewing your document 75

Part V: Working the Web with
Internet Explorer 5 77

Adding a Web Page to Your Links Bar 78
Bookmarking a Web Page 78
Browsing Web Pages Offline 79
Changing Fonts and Background Colors 80
Changing the Toolbar 81
Choosing Your Home Page 82
Copying Information from a Web Page 83
Creating a Shortcut to a Web Page 83
Displaying Web Pages Faster 83
Finding What You Want on the Web 83
Printing a Web Page 84
Saving a Web Page 85
Sending a Web Page in E-Mail 86
Using a Web Page as Desktop Wallpaper 87
Viewing Web Pages Offline 87

Part VI: Using Outlook Express E-Mail
and News 89

Adding a Mail or News Account 90
Adding Contacts from Outlook Express 93
Adding Contacts to Your Address Book 93
Adding Folders 94
Assigning Importance to a Message 94
Checking Spelling in a Message 95
Copying Messages 95
Creating a Business Card 95
Deleting a Mail Message 97
Deleting Folders 97
Forwarding a Mail Message 97
Moving Messages 97
Opening an Attachment 98
Opening the Address Book 98
Posting Messages to Newsgroups 98
Printing a Message 99
Reading Mail Messages 99
Replying to a Mail Message 99

Replying to Newsgroup Messages 99
Saving a Copy of a Message 100
Saving a File Attachment 100
Sending a File in a Message 100
Sending a Picture in a Message 100
Sending E-Mail Messages 101
Sending Messages on Stationery 101

Part VII: Print (ing) or Perish *105*

Adding a Printer to Your Computer 106
Canceling the Printing of a Document 110
Changing the Order of Documents Waiting to Print 111
Pausing the Printing of a Document 112
Printing a Document 112
Printing More Than One Copy 112
Printing Multiple Pages on a Sheet 113
Printing on Both Sides of the Paper 114
Restarting the Printing of a Document 114
Selecting Paper Size 115
Setting Page Orientation 115
Setting Printer Resolution 116
Using a Separator Page 116
Viewing Documents Waiting to Print 117

Part VIII: Networking Near and Far *119*

Browsing Your Network 120
Connecting to Another Computer 121
Connecting to Printers on Your Network 125
Connecting to the Internet 128
Creating a Dial-up Connection 128
Disconnecting from the Network 129
Finding Printers on the Network 130
Serving Incoming Connections 130
    Setting sharing permissions for drives and folders 134
    Setting up File and Printer Sharing 136
    Setting up printer-sharing permissions 136
    Sharing your files or folders on the network 138
    Sharing your printer on the network 139
    Turning off folder sharing 141
    Turning off printer sharing 142

Part IX: Personalizing Your Computer *143*

Adding Toolbar Buttons in Folder Windows 144
Adjusting Keyboard Response 145
Adjusting Keystroke Response 146
Adjusting Screen Contrast 147
Assigning Sounds to Program Events 148

Changing the System Sound Volume 148
Changing Screen Resolution 149
Changing the Appearance of Folder Items 150
Changing the Look of Desktop Items 150
Creating a Sound Scheme 151
Customizing a Desktop Pattern 151
Displaying Captions 152
Getting Visual System Warnings 153
Making Folders Look Like Web Pages 153
Making the Keyboard Act Like a Mouse 154
Opening Folders in Their Own Windows 154
Setting a Desktop Background 155
Setting a Screen Saver 155
ToggleKeys 156
Using the Active Desktop Feature 156

Glossary: Techie Talk *157*

Index *163*

Book Registration Information ......*Back of Book*

How to Use This Book

Welcome to *Windows 2000 Professional For Dummies Quick Reference,* a guide designed to make life with Windows 2000 Professional quicker and easier. This book gives you just what you need to run Windows 2000 Professional and get your work done.

Keep this book at your side for those times when you need quick steps for performing a new task or a handy refresher for a procedure you've forgotten.

How This Book Is Organized

This book is divided into ten parts.

Part I: Getting to Know Windows 2000

Part I of this book provides you with the basic information you need to get started, including how to start and quit Windows 2000. This part helps you find your way around the desktop, the display area that serves as a launch point for most of your work with Windows 2000. Along the way, you discover the commands, menus, and dialog boxes that put you in control of your Windows 2000 program. If you hit a stumbling block, help is only a mouse click or keystroke away; this part also introduces you to the easy-to-use Help program.

Part II: Working with Files and Folders

Part II explains everything you need to know about organizing electronic files and folders with Windows 2000. You find out how to create folders for your files, as well as how to find, open, move, copy, and delete files.

Part III: Working with Programs

You have to have them. Countless programs run under Windows 2000, and you need to know how to add them to your system, how to start them, and how to get out of them. Part III tells you the basics of what you need to know to make your programs work for you.

Part IV: Using All Those Accessories

Believe it or not, Windows ships with lots of free software. Here's where to look for it.

Part V: Working the Web with Internet Explorer 5

Internet Explorer 5 is an easy and powerful tool for accessing the World Wide Web. Part V shows you how to use IE 5 to get "out on the Net" and work the Web.

Part VI: Using Outlook Express E-Mail and News

Part VI focuses on using Windows 2000 to communicate with the outside world. You discover how to create and send e-mail messages, as well as print and save your messages. If you want to attach documents to your e-mail, this part provides easy steps.

Part VII: Print (ing) or Perish

You either print or perish. Use this part to help get your works out of the computer. Here's where you can find information on printing documents and controlling your printer.

Part VIII: Networking Near and Far

Your office space is virtually unlimited when you have the ability to network across time and space. In this part, you discover how to connect to computers in your network, connect to printers on your network, and share your printer. You also find out how to browse your workgroup or domain.

Part IX: Personalizing Your Computer

This part tells you how to put the word "personal" back in your computer. You'll learn how to change the appearance and the way certain features work in the operating system to make it more to your liking.

Glossary: Techie Talk

Just when you thought you were used to the lingo, Windows 2000 pops up with some additions. Techie Talk tells you the words you need to know and what they mean.

The Cast of Icons

This icon alerts you to useful information or helpful shortcuts that make using Windows 2000 easier.

To avoid potential problems, read the information marked with this icon and proceed with caution.

This icon flags a common problem associated with a particular task or a feature that may not work as expected.

Read the information marked with this icon to find out the quickest way to accomplish a task.

Do you need more information on a particular topic? This icon points you to a useful section of the book *Windows 2000 Professional For Dummies,* written by Andy Rathbone and published by IDG Books Worldwide, Inc.

Getting to Know Windows 2000

If you're a new Windows user, look in this part for the basics of using Windows 2000 (and most other Windows systems).

If you're migrating from Windows 95 or Windows 98, you can probably skip this part — it's old news.

In this part . . .

- ✔ Changing file and folder names
- ✔ Making copies of your files
- ✔ Creating folders to hold your files
- ✔ Removing unwanted files and folders
- ✔ Finding files
- ✔ Moving files and folders to safe places
- ✔ Opening files

 *Part 1*

Desktop

When you start Windows 2000 Professional, you see a large display area called the *desktop*. The desktop can hold a lot of different elements, many of which appear as an icon of some sort.

 An *icon* is nothing more than a cute little picture that represents something else. In Windows 2000 Professional, icons represent things like programs, folders, and documents.

The desktop acts like a conventional desk on which you place the items you work with throughout the day. It's the starting point for most of your interactions with Windows 2000 Professional.

As you survey the desktop, you see the following items:

What You See	What It Is	What It's For
▣	My Computer	You can use My Computer to see everything on your computer quickly and easily. Double-click the My Computer icon on the desktop to browse through your files and folders.
▩	My Network Places	If you are using a network, the My Network Places icon appears on your desktop. Double-click it to browse through the computers in your workgroup or domain and the computers on your entire network.
▨	Internet Explorer	A quick click on this icon will speed you on your way to the Internet. With Internet Explorer and an Internet connection, you can search and explore the World Wide Web.
▢	My Documents	A handy desktop folder where you can store documents, graphics, or any other files that you want to access quickly.
▧	Recycle Bin	When you delete files, Windows 2000 Professional Explorer doesn't just remove them from your disk. If you're deleting files from a hard disk, Windows 2000 Professional Explorer moves the files to a special folder called the Recycle Bin so that you can retrieve the files later if you want.
▦	Start button	At the bottom of your screen is the Windows Taskbar. It contains the Start button, which you can use to start a program or find a file quickly. When you open a program, document, or window, a button appears on the taskbar. You can use these buttons to switch between the open windows quickly.

What You See	What It Is	What It's For
	Shortcut icons	Windows 2000 Professional lets you add icons for commonly used programs, documents, folders, and other items to the desktop. If these icons appear on your desktop, you can launch programs or open documents or folders by double-clicking their shortcut icons.

Dialog Boxes

A *dialog box* is simply an on-screen form that you fill out to tell Windows 2000 Professional how to process a command.

✦ Any time Windows 2000 Professional needs information on how to proceed, a dialog box asks for information.

✦ Any time you see a menu command followed by an ellipsis — little dots that look like this . . . — you know that a dialog box appears when you choose that command.

✦ If Windows 2000 Professional requires more information or a decision from you, the dialog box has *buttons*.

TIP

Windows 2000 Professional often displays *messages* or *warnings* in the guise of a dialog box. Sometimes the dialog box is simply a message informing you of possible consequences of a command action.

✦ To dismiss a message, click OK.

✦ If the message contains two or more command buttons:

• Click OK to proceed.

• Click Cancel to cancel the action and dismiss the message.

Closing a dialog box

To close a dialog box, try one of the following methods:

✦ Click Cancel.

✦ Click the Close button (the X button in the upper-right corner of the dialog box).

✦ Press the Esc button on your keyboard.

Making selections

To make selections within a dialog box:

1. Select options or type text to specify the information you want in a dialog box.

Click an option to select it or press Alt plus the underlined letter in the option name.

 If an item in a dialog box is dimmed, it is unavailable because it requires a selection or some previous action.

 If you don't know what an option does, press F1 or click the Help button to see a description of the options.

2. When you finish with the dialog box, choose the appropriate command button to carry out the command.

Usually, clicking OK carries out the command. Sometimes the button that carries out the command has a label, such as Open or Find Next.

When you choose option buttons and check boxes:

✦ Click an option button to select it. Any other option in the group turns off automatically. (You can select only one option button in a group.)

 A selected option button contains a dot.

✦ Click a check box to turn that option on or off. You can select as many check boxes as you want. (Check boxes don't turn off automatically when you click other check boxes.)

TIP

A selected check box contains a check mark.

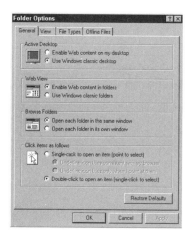

When you choose command buttons:

✦ Another dialog box appears if you choose a button with an ellipsis.

✦ The dialog box expands if you choose a button with double arrows.

When you choose list boxes:

✦ Click an item in any kind of list to select it or scroll, if you see arrows, to see more items.

✦ In a *drop-down* list box, which shows a list of items to choose from, click the arrow to display a list of options to select.

✦ In some lists, you can select more than one item. In such a list, click a selection a second time to turn it off.

When you choose miscellaneous items, you can type, edit, and paste text in any text box. If a text box contains text when you move to it, all the text is selected, and any text you type replaces it. Press Delete or Backspace to delete the text and start from scratch.

Help!

Online help is only a mouse click or keystroke away from wherever you are in Windows 2000 Professional. When in doubt, simply look up the topic in Help. You can access help by selecting Help from the menu bar in any window, pressing F1, or choosing Help from the Start button.

The following table shows what you can do (and how you can do it) in the Help window:

What You Can Do	How You Do It
Go back to a previous topic	Click the Back button or click the Help Topics button to return to the Contents tab of Help and select another subject. If a Display History window appears in Help, you can select a previous help item from the History window.
Jump to another Help topic	Click the underlined jump term. You can also click the Help Topics button and then select another topic. Many Help windows have a Related Topics button at the end of the Help text that you can click for information on related items, too.
Display a definition	Click a term with dotted underlining and then click anywhere on-screen to close the definition.
Minimize Help to an icon	Click the Minimize button in the Help window.
Exit Help	Click the Close button.

Finding a topic in Help

To find a topic in the Windows 2000 Professional Help system, try one of the following methods:

+ Click the Contents tab to see topics by category.

+ Click the Index tab to see a list of entries. You can either type the word you're looking for or scroll through the list of entries.

+ Click the Find tab to search for words or phrases.

Getting information on dialog box settings

To get Help on each item in a dialog box:

1. Click the question-mark button at the top of a dialog box.

   If the dialog box doesn't have this button, look for a Help button or try pressing F1.

2. Click the item you want information about. A pop-up window appears.

3. If you want to print or copy the information in a pop-up window, right-click inside the window and then click Print Topic.

4. To close the pop-up window, click inside it.

Another way to get Help on an item on-screen is to use your right mouse button to click the area that you want Help on and then click the What's This? command.

Printing a Help topic

To print a Help topic, try one of the following methods:

✦ In the Help topic you want to print, click the Print button or the Options button (which button appears depends on where you have accessed Help from) and then click Print Topic.

✦ Right-click inside the Help window and then click Print Topic on the pop-up menu.

You can print a group of related topics by clicking the appropriate book icon in the Help Contents windows and then clicking Print.

To print the help in a pop-up window, right-click inside the pop-up window and then click Print Topic.

Searching for Help with Search

To search for a topic by using the Search dialog box:

1. In the Help Topics window, click the Search tab to display the Search window.

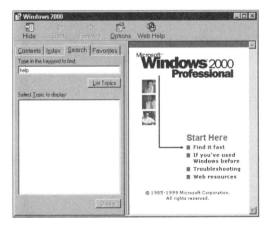

2. In the Search window, type the word or phrase you're looking for.

3. Select a word or phrase that matches the topic you're searching for in the Select Topic to Display list.

4. In the bottom list box, click the topic titles that are relevant to your search and then click the Display button to view the topic.

Starting Help

To start Help, try one of the following methods:

✦ Press F1 wherever you are working.

✦ Click the Start button on the taskbar and then click Help.

In either case, the Help Topic: Windows 2000 Professional Help dialog box appears. The Help Contents window lists the major topics for Windows 2000 Professional. From this window, you can move to more-specific information by clicking the Contents, Find, or Index tabs. To see a list of index entries in any tab, either type the word you're looking for or scroll through the list.

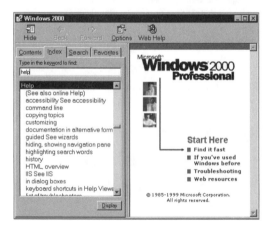

Using the Help Contents

When the Help system first starts, the Help Topics: Windows 2000 Professional dialog box appears with the Contents tab showing. The Contents tab displays the table of contents for the Help system in sections represented by icons that look like books.

To see a list of topics in a Help book:

1. Click the book.

2. Click the Open button to view the topics in the book.

To read a topic from the list in a Help book:

1. Click the topic.

2. Click the Display button.

Mousing Around

Windows 2000 Professional often requires you to use the mouse in different ways, depending on the task at hand. You can click, double-click, right-click, or drag.

Clicking

Clicking is the mouse action you'll probably use the most. To click means that you point the mouse pointer at an object and click the *left* (primary) mouse button.

If you're left-handed and have your mouse set up so that the right mouse button is the primary button, then click the right button.

Double-clicking

Double-clicking means to click the primary (left) mouse button two times — fast.

You need a steady hand to master this action because you have to click twice without moving the mouse.

Dragging

Dragging moves an on-screen object from one place to another.

1. Point to an object.

2. Press and hold the primary (left) mouse button.

3. Move the mouse to move the object to another location on the screen.

4. When the object is where you want it on the screen, release the mouse button.

Right-clicking

Right-clicking means to point to an object and click the right mouse button (the left mouse button for you lefties who have the right button set as the primary button). Right-clicking works like clicking, but you use a different button and get a different result.

Usually, a shortcut menu pops up when you right-click an object.

Selecting Items

In the world of Windows 2000, you must specify an object (disk, file, folder) for a command to act upon. Whether the disk, file, or folder is on your desktop or in Windows Explorer, you have to point out the object of your desire.

Selecting disks

To select a disk, click the disk icon.

Selecting files

To select a file:

1. Make sure that the folder containing the file is active (appears open).

2. Scroll through the file pane until you see the file.

3. Click the file.

 You can select adjacent files by clicking the first file and then pressing the Shift key while you click the last file. If you need to select files that aren't adjacent, hold down the Ctrl key while you click one file at a time.

Selecting folders

To select a folder, scroll through the folder pane until you see the folder and then click the folder.

 If the folder is a subfolder of another folder, you may need to expand the parent folder by double-clicking it in order to see the subfolder.

Shutting Down Windows 2000 Professional

Stop! Don't touch that power switch until you read this section. Windows 2000 Professional must be allowed to shut down gracefully.

To shut down your computer:

1. Click the Start button. The Start menu appears.

2. Point to Shut Down and then select Shut Down in the Shut Down Windows dialog box.

WARNING

Don't turn off your computer yet!

3. Wait until a message appears telling you that it is now safe to turn off your computer.

4. Switch off your computer.

Start Menu

The Start menu appears when you click the Start button located at the lower-left side of the screen.

You can add or remove items from the Start menu or its submenus.

What It Is	*What It's For*
Programs	Displays the Programs menu, which lists any Programs submenus including the MS-DOS Prompt and Windows 2000 Professional Explorer.
Documents	Displays a list of up to the last 15 documents you've used. You can open any of the documents on the list by simply clicking the document's name.
Settings	Displays the Settings submenu.
Control Panel	Displays the Control Panel applet.
Printers	Displays the Printers window so that you can add a new printer, modify an existing printer, or view documents being printed.
Taskbar	Displays the Taskbar Properties dialog box so that you can change the way the taskbar works.
Find	Displays the Find submenu.
Files or Computers	Displays the Find: All Files dialog box so that you can search for files or folders.
Computer	Displays the Find: Computer dialog box so that you can search for computers on a network.
Help	Displays the Help Topics window so that you can get help with commands and procedures.
Run	Displays the Run dialog box, which you can use to start programs.
Shut Down	Displays the Shut Down dialog box so that you can exit Windows 2000 Professional.

Starting Windows 2000 Professional

Windows 2000 Professional is a secure system, kind of like your bank's ATM — you have to log on to let it know you're you. You won't be able to compute until you get past Windows 2000 Professional's first line of defense, the Welcome box.

You must identify yourself and enter your password each time you start Windows 2000 Professional.

To start Windows 2000 Professional:

1. Turn on your computer.

2. When the logon message appears, press Ctrl+Alt+Delete to log on.

If your computer is set up to start more than one operating system, use your mouse to press an arrow key at the start-up screen to choose Windows 2000 Professional and then press Enter.

Even if you see a message already displayed that asks you to enter your password, always press Ctrl+Alt+Delete before you type your password. The Ctrl+Alt+Delete sequence ensures the security of your system.

3. In the Welcome dialog box, type your username — your name will work fine — and password.

If you're starting Windows 2000 Professional for the first time and do not already have a password, simply enter a password and confirm it by entering it again when Windows 2000 Professional asks.

4. Select either your local computer name or the name of a Windows 2000 Server domain as designated by your system administrator.

5. Click OK.

As soon as you log on, you can run applications, share files with other users on the network, connect to a printer, and control who has access to your computer and its files.

Window Parts

Program windows resemble sheets of paper on your conventional desk. In Windows 2000, program windows display program elements and contents. You can arrange, resize, and move program windows around on your screen.

Control-menu commands

Control-menu commands appear on the Control menus of program windows, document windows, and some dialog boxes.

To activate the Control menu of a window or dialog box, click the Control-menu button located in the upper-left corner of the window or dialog box.

The Control-menu commands let you manipulate a window or dialog box in some of the following ways:

Click This Command	To Do This
Restore	Undo the last Minimize or Maximize command.
Move	Tell Windows 2000 Professional that you want to move the application window. When you click this command, the pointer changes to a four-headed arrow. You move the window by using the cursor direction keys on your keyboard to indicate the direction in which you want the window to move. Press Enter when you're finished.
Size	Tell Windows 2000 Professional that you want to change the size of the application window. When you click this command, the pointer changes to a four-headed arrow. You change the window size by using the cursor direction keys on your keyboard to extend or shrink the window's border. Press Enter when finished.
Minimize	Tell Windows 2000 Professional that you want to remove the application window from the screen. Windows 2000 Professional hides the application window and leaves its icon on the taskbar as a reminder that the application is active.
Maximize	Tell Windows 2000 Professional that you want the application window to expand and fill up the entire screen.
Close	Close the window and, consequently, the application itself. If you close a document window, you also close the document. If you haven't saved the document, you may lose your work. Most applications ask, however, whether you want to save the document or file before closing it.

The commands available on the Control menu vary for different applications, but most Control menus include at least the Move and Close commands.

Menus

All Windows-based applications group commands into sets called *menus,* which are displayed in the *menu bar* across the top of the application window. Menus vary in each application, but most applications include at least a File menu, an Edit menu, and a Help menu.

To choose a menu command:

1. Choose the menu name in the menu bar and hold down the mouse button.

2. Drag to select the command you want and then release the mouse button.

You can also activate the command by pressing the Alt key and the underlined letter in the menu name.

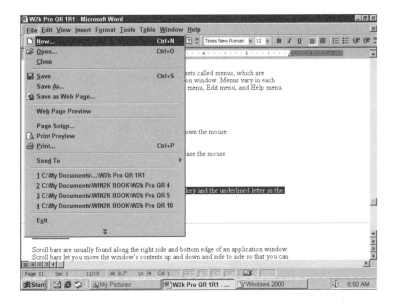

Scroll bars

Scroll bars are usually found along the right side and bottom edge of an application window. Scroll bars let you move the window's contents up and down and side to side so that you can see a document or some data that's too long or wide to fit entirely within the window.

To use the mouse to manipulate the scroll bar, choose one of the following methods:

✦ Click the arrow at either end of the scroll bar to move in the direction of the arrow.

✦ Grab the scroll box and drag it in the direction you want to move.

✦ Simply click on the scroll bar above or below the scroll box in the direction that you want the window to move.

Shortcut menus

Shortcut menus are a new feature that found their way first into Windows 95 and are also in Windows 2000 Professional. The idea is that many applications have enough intelligence to know what commands are needed in a given situation. These applications present often-used commands in shortcut menus.

To display a shortcut menu, right-click the object you want to manipulate. Then click the desired command from the shortcut menu.

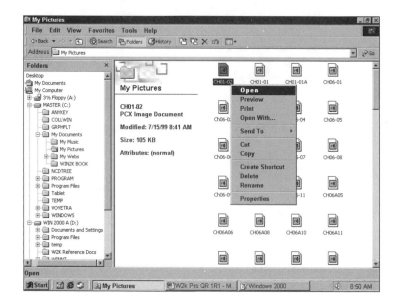

For example, if you right-click a file or folder, the menu that appears shows the most frequently used commands for that file or folder.

Title bars

Title bars live at the top of a program window. They provide information about the program. For example, title bars tell you

+ What application you're currently running.

+ The name of the document showing in the document window.

This is really handy if you forget what program you're working in and what it is that you're working on.

Toolbars

Toolbars are the rows of buttons, boxes, or icons that sometimes appear immediately beneath a program's menu bar, representing shortcuts to tools. Toolbar buttons provide shortcuts for activating certain menu commands. To activate a Toolbar button, simply click the button.

Window buttons

Look around the edges of a Windows-based program, and you see buttons and icons. You use buttons and icons to display the Control menu (as I describe for the Control-menu commands in this part), to close an application, and to minimize or resize an application's window.

Click This Button	To Do This
Program button	Display the application's Control menu
Document button	Display the document's Control menu
Minimize button	Shrink a window down to an icon on the taskbar
Restore button	Restore a window to its previous size
Maximize button	Enlarge a window to fill the screen
Close button	Close the application and any documents opened within the application

Part II

Working with Files and Folders

Whether you know it or not, you create files of some type every time you work with your computer. They come from your word-processing program, your spreadsheet program, your e-mail program, and your Internet programs. As files begin to proliferate and accumulate, knowing how to care for them becomes more and more important. In this part, you find out how to do important things to your files, like deleting, renaming, copying, and moving them.

In this part . . .

- ✔ Changing file and folder names
- ✔ Making copies of your files
- ✔ Creating folders to hold your files
- ✔ Removing unwanted files and folders
- ✔ Finding files
- ✔ Moving files and folders to safe places
- ✔ Opening files

Associating File Types

Windows 2000 Professional is smart enough to open a file with the corresponding application as long as you tell it *what* goes *where* and *why*. For example, Microsoft Word 2000 for Windows creates files with .DOC as the filename extension. Windows 2000 Professional launches Word for Windows whenever you open a file with the .DOC extension, provided that you have told Windows 2000 which program files with the .DOC extension belong to.

Follow these steps to tell Windows 2000 Professional which application opens a certain type of file:

1. Choose Start⇨Programs⇨Accessories⇨Windows Explorer to open Windows Explorer.

2. Click Tools⇨Folder Options.

3. Click the File Types tab.

4. Click New.

5. Type a new or existing filename extension and then click Advanced.

6. In File Type, click New to associate a new file type with the filename extension. Or click one of the existing file types from the list.

To change the program that opens a file, click Change on the File Types tab.

Changing a File or Folder Name

One of the best features of Windows is that it enables you to give files meaningful names. No more XYZFODO.DOC like in the days of DOS, an operating system that could only tolerate 8 characters (plus three for the extension) in a filename. Now you can call the file what it is — "My Blockbuster Screenplay." And if you don't like that name, change it.

Here's how to change the name of a file or folder:

1. In My Computer or Windows Explorer, click the file or folder that you want to rename. You don't need to open it.

2. Choose File⇨Rename. The current file or folder name appears highlighted. Or right-click the file and choose Rename from the menu.

3. Type the new name (up to 255 characters, including spaces) and then press Enter.

Note: You can be creative with filenames as long as you don't use characters like these: \ / * ? " < > |

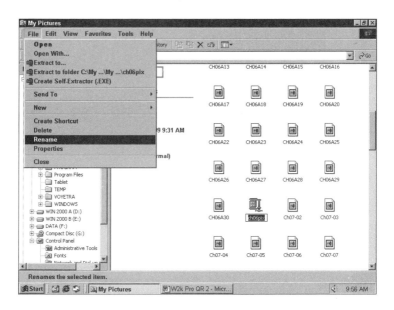

Changing the Recycle Bin's Size

The Recycle bin takes up space (bytes) on your hard drive, so you may want to control the amount of disk space it can use.

1. Right-click the Recycle Bin icon on the desktop and choose Properties from the menu. The Recycle Bin Properties dialog box appears.

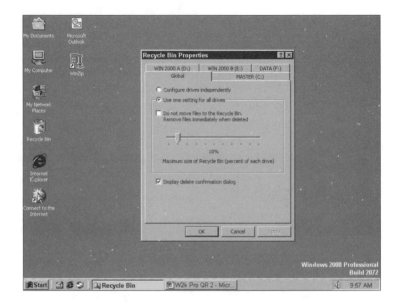

2. Click the Global tab if you have the Use One Setting for All Drives option checked. Or, to set the Recycle Bin size for individual drives, check the Configure Drives Independently option and then click the Disk tab to set the size for that particular drive.

3. Drag the slider control to increase or decrease the amount of disk space you want to reserve for storing deleted files.

You can control the size of each Recycle Bin on each of your drives:

✦ To use different settings for different drives, select the Configure Drives Independently option button and then click the tab of the drive whose settings you want to change.

✦ If you want to use the same settings for all drives, select the Use One Setting for All Drives option button.

Copying a File to a Disk

To copy a file or folder to a floppy disk, follow these steps:

1. Insert the floppy disk into the disk drive.

2. Choose Start⇨Programs⇨Accessories⇨Windows Explorer to open Windows Explorer.

3. Click the file or folder you want to copy.

4. Choose File⇨Send To⇨3½ Floppy (A).

 You can also copy a file or folder to a floppy disk by right-clicking the file or folder and choosing Send To⇨3½ Floppy (A).

Copying Files or Folders

One copy of a file is never enough. Your boss wants a copy, your best friend needs a copy, and so on. Even more important is that you need a copy. If you remember only one thing from this section of the book, make it the word *backup*. No, I don't mean work in reverse. I mean keep duplicate copies of your important files. You have several ways to copy files or folders, so you have no excuse for not having copies of important files.

Using the mouse to drag and drop a copy

Follow these steps to copy a file or folder by using the mouse:

1. Choose Start⇨Programs⇨Accessories⇨Windows Explorer to open Windows Explorer.

2. Click the icon of the disk drive that contains the file or folder you want to copy.

3. If you want to copy the folder and its entire contents, click the folder. If you want to copy a file within a folder, click the file in the Windows Explorer file pane.

4. Drag the file or folder to the icon of the disk drive to which you want to copy the file or folder.

Here's how to copy a file or folder to another folder on the same hard disk by using the mouse:

1. Click the icon of the disk drive that contains the file or folder you want to copy.

2. Click the file or folder that you want to copy. If you want to copy the folder and its entire contents, click the folder. If you want to copy a file within a folder, click the file in the Explorer file pane.

3. Hold down the Ctrl key and drag the folder or file to the folder to which you want to copy the file.

Using the menu to copy a file or folder

Here's how to copy a file or folder by using the menu:

1. Click the icon of the disk drive that contains the file or folder you want to copy.

2. Click the file or folder you want to copy. If you want to copy the folder and its entire contents, click the folder. If you want to copy a file within a folder, click the file in the Explorer file pane.

3. Copy the file or folder by choosing Edit⇨Copy.

4. Open the folder or disk where you want to put the copy.

5. Paste the file or folder by choosing Edit⇨Paste.

To select more than one file or folder to copy, hold down the Ctrl key and then click the items you want.

You can also use the Copy to Folder command. Here's how:

1. Click the icon of the disk drive that contains the file or folder you want to copy.

2. Click the file or folder you want to copy. If you want to copy the folder and its entire contents, click the folder. If you want to copy a file within a folder, click the file in the Explorer file pane.

3. Copy the file or folder by choosing Edit⇨Copy to Folder.

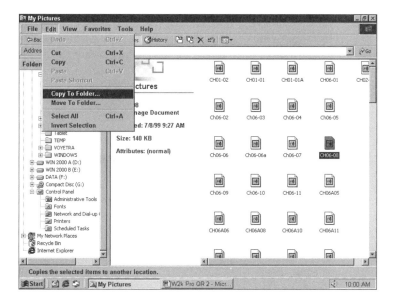

4. In the Browse for Folder dialog box, select the folder or disk where you want to put the copy.

5. Click OK.

Creating Folders

Just like the cardboard file folders that you cram paper documents into at your desk, folders on your Windows 2000 Professional desktop help to organize and manage data, software, and other files on your computer system.

Follow these steps to create a new folder:

1. Open My Computer or Windows Explorer and select the disk drive or open the folder in which you want to create a new folder.

2. Choose File➪New➪Folder. The new folder appears with the temporary name New Folder.

3. Type a name for the new folder and then press Enter.

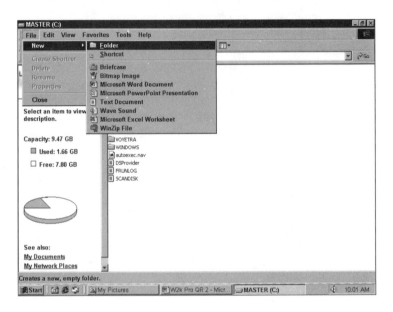

Deleting a File or Folder

If your productivity were measured by the number of documents and files you create on any given day, you'd probably be in line for a huge pay increase. Chances are that your boss would discover that your productivity quotient was way too high and you would be asked to clean out old and unused documents or files to make room for "real" work.

Follow these steps to delete a file:

1. In Windows Explorer, click the file or folder that you want to delete. If you want to delete a folder and its entire contents, click the folder. If you want to delete a file within a folder, click the file in the Explorer file pane.

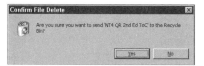

2. Choose File⇨Delete. The Confirm File Delete message box appears.

3. Confirm that you do want to delete the file or folder. Windows 2000 Professional Explorer then deletes it.

TIP

If the file is on a hard disk, Windows 2000 Professional also places it in the Recycle Bin. **See also** "Recycle Bin," later in this part.

Emptying the Recycle Bin

Here's how to empty the Recycle Bin:

1. Double-click the Recycle Bin icon on the desktop.

2. Click the Empty Recycle Bin button or choose File⇨Empty Recycle Bin.

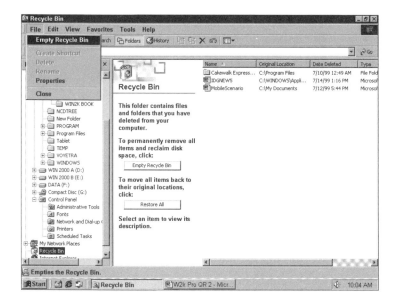

TIP

If you want to remove only some of the items in the Recycle Bin, hold the Ctrl key while clicking each item. Then choose File⇨Delete.

Finding a File or Folder

You know that you're creating them. Sure, you know they're on your hard drive, but can you find them? And find them you must because before you can copy them, delete them, move them, or rename them, you have to find them.

Here's how to find a file or folder using the Search command on the Start menu:

1. Click the Start button. The Start menu appears.

2. Point to Search to display the Search submenu.

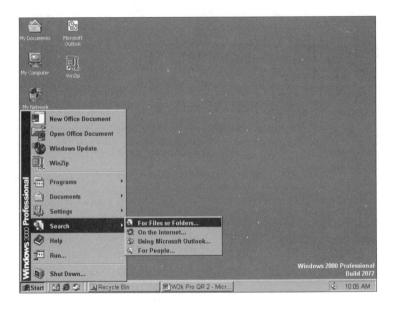

3. Choose Files or Folders from the menu. The Find: All Files dialog box appears.

4. In the Search for files or folders named box, type all or part of the filename. Don't panic if you don't know the name of a file; you can refine the search by clicking search options and specifying a Date, Time, Size, or Advanced options and specifying the appropriate information.

If you want to specify where Windows should begin its search, click Look In to display the Browse for Folder dialog box and select the folder where you want to begin the search.

5. Click Search Now to begin the search.

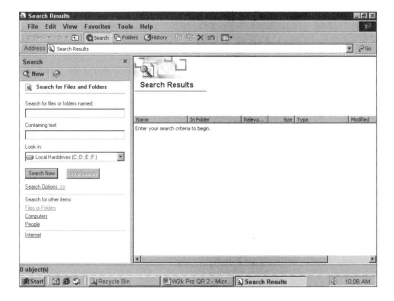

If you find yourself searching for the same files or types of files again and again, you can save the search results. Here's how:

1. Search for files as described in the previous set of steps.

2. Choose File⇨Save Search. Windows places an icon representing the search results or search criteria on your desktop or in the folder of your choice.

After you double-click the search results icon, you can restart the search or update the search results by clicking Find Now.

Moving Files or Folders

When you want to reorganize files or folders, you'll usually move them to new locations in Windows Explorer using one of the methods that follows.

Using the mouse

To move a file or folder to another folder on your hard disk by using the mouse, follow these steps:

1. Choose Start⇨Programs⇨Accessories⇨Windows Explorer.

2. Click the icon of the disk drive that contains the file or folder that you want to move.

3. Click the file or folder you want to move. If you want to move a folder and its entire contents, click the folder. If you want to move a file within a folder, click the file in the Explorer file pane.

4. Drag the folder or file to the folder on the hard drive to which you want to move the folder or file.

Using menu commands

Here's how to move a file or folder by using menu commands:

1. In Explorer, click the icon of the disk drive that contains the file or folder you want to move.

2. Click the file or folder that you want to move. If you want to move a folder and its entire contents, click the folder. If you want to move a file within a folder, click the file in the Explorer file pane.

3. Choose Edit⇨Cut.

4. Click the icon of the disk drive to which you want to move the file or folder.

5. Click the folder to which you want to move the file.

6. Choose Edit⇨Paste.

Follow these steps to copy a file or folder by choosing Edit⇨Move to Folder:

1. Click the icon of the disk drive that contains the file or folder you want to copy.

2. Click the file or folder you want to copy. If you want to copy the folder and its entire contents, click the folder. If you want to copy a file within a folder, click the file in the Explorer file pane.

3. Copy the file or folder by choosing Edit⇨Move to Folder.

4. In the Browse for Folder dialog box, select the folder or disk where you want to put the copy.

5. Click OK.

My Documents Folder

My Documents is a folder that provides you with a convenient place to store documents, graphics, or other files you want to access quickly. On your desktop, it's represented by a folder with a sheet of paper in it. When you save a file in a program such as WordPad or Paint, the file is automatically saved in My Documents unless you choose a different location.

To change the default folder for My Documents, right-click My Documents, click Properties, and, in Target, type or browse for the path and folder name where you want to save files.

If you set file preview options in Excel or PowerPoint, you can select a file in My Documents and preview it in the left pane of Windows Explorer when My Documents is in Web view.

Opening a File

Flexibility is the key to gaining oneness with Windows 2000 Professional. You may find that Windows 2000 is very flexible, enabling you to be flexible too. Sometimes, you may launch an application program, like your favorite word-processing program, and then use it to open a file to work on. Other times you may have the file itself in your sights and may want to open your word-processing program with that file as the active document. This is what I call the *outside in* approach. Very flexible.

Here's how to open a file from Explorer:

1. In Explorer, click the icon of the disk drive that contains the file you want to open.

2. Click the file you want to open.

3. Choose File⇨Open to open the file.

Recycle Bin

The Recycle Bin is a welcome sight for those users who often delete the wrong files or simply decide that they want to use a file that they've deleted. Recycle Bin only works with files deleted from Windows 2000 Professional Explorer.

Removing Files Permanently When You Delete Them

In the old days, hitting the Delete key could send you into a serious state of panic if you had your cursor parked over the wrong folder or file. Fear not! Windows 2000 Professional has a safety net called the Recycle Bin. Instead of sending files to Nevernever Land when you hit Delete, Windows 2000 Professional moves the files to the Recycle Bin where they continue to live, in a dormant state, on your hard disk.

Here's how to make sure that the Recycle Bin is ready to recycle:

1. Using your right mouse button, click the Recycle Bin icon on the desktop and then point to Properties on the menu.

Retrieving Deleted Files or Shortcuts

2. Make sure that the Do not move files to the Recycle Bin check box is unchecked.

If you have no fear and like to work without a net, you can set the Recycle Bin so that it doesn't hold on to files when you delete them. Simply check the Do not move files to the Recycle Bin box in Step 2 above.

Note, however, that if you select this box, you can't recover any files you delete.

Files deleted from network locations, diskettes, Zip disks, and so on are not copied to the Recycle Bin. Windows 2000 Professional permanently removes them when you delete them. (*See also* the "Recycle Bin" section, earlier in this part.)

Retrieving Deleted Files or Shortcuts

You can and will at some point delete a file that you didn't mean to delete. The good news is that you can get the file back if you have the Recycle Bin activated.

Follow these steps to retrieve a file or shortcut from the Recycle Bin:

1. Double-click the Recycle Bin icon on the desktop.

2. Click the file or shortcut that you want to retrieve.

3. Click the Restore button.

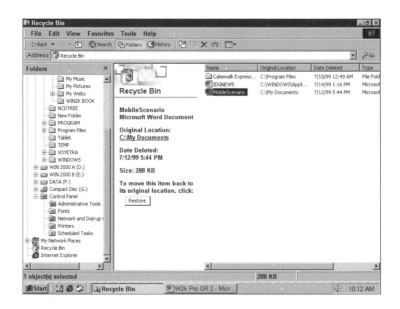

If you restore a file that was originally located in a deleted folder, Windows recreates the folder and then restores the file to it.

Sending Files to Other Places

You can send a file to a disk drive, an e-mail program, a fax program, the desktop, the Briefcase, and a slew of other places depending on what kinds of application programs you have on your system. And you can do it quickly and painlessly with the Send To command.

To quickly send files to another place, follow these steps:

1. Right-click the file you want to send.

2. Point to Send To, and then click the destination.

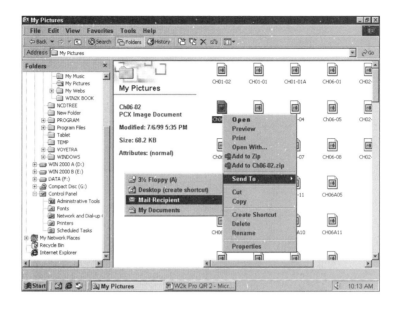

 Want more destinations? You can add other destinations to the Send To command. In the Send To folder, located in your Windows folder, create shortcuts to the destinations you send files to often; for example, a printer, fax, or particular folder.

Sorting Files

You can sort the files that you're viewing in different ways. Here's how to sort a list of files or directories:

1. In Explorer, select the drive and directory you want to view.

2. Choose View⇨Arrange Icons to view its submenu.

3. From the submenu, choose how you want to sort the list of files or directories. Your choices are as follows:

- by Name
- by Type
- by Size
- by Date

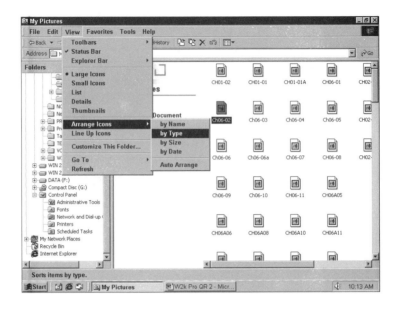

Or, in Explorer, click the column heading that you want to use to sort. For example, to sort by date, click the Modified column heading.

Viewing a File's Properties

Each file has properties. *Properties* are things such as the date and time the file was created, when the file was last accessed or changed, and other information. You can also change attributes of a file. (For example, you can make the file a read-only file.)

To view a file's properties, follow these steps:

1. Choose Start⇨Programs⇨Accessories⇨Windows Explorer to open Windows Explorer.

2. Select the file whose properties you want to view.

3. Choose File⇨Properties. The Properties dialog box for that file appears.

Tabs appear in the file's Properties dialog box.

The General tab displays the filename, the file type (such as an application), the file location, and the file size. Also displayed in this tab is the MS-DOS name (which is important if the file has a long name) and the date that the file was created, modified, or accessed last. The tab also lists three attributes that you can modify for the file: Read-only, Hidden, and Archive.

Each type of file that you view the properties for may render different tabs. For example, if you view the properties of a graphic file, such as a bitmap file, the tab that you need is the Image tab. With this tab, you can preview the file.

Viewing Files

To view a list of files, follow these steps:

1. Choose Start⇨Programs⇨Accessories⇨Windows Explorer to open Windows Explorer.

2. Select the disk drive containing the files or directories you want to view.

3. Select the directory containing the files or directories you want to view.

Viewing Graphics Files

If pictures (clip art, wallpaper, icons, and so on) are your thing, you can view quickie view, or *thumbnail*, versions of graphic files.

1. In My Computer or Explorer, click the folder that contains the graphics files you want to view as thumbnails.

2. Choose View⇨Thumbnails.

Windows Explorer

Every now and then, you need to see what's on your computer. After all, you work so hard creating all those files that seeing them on your hard drive is reassurance that your efforts are not in vain. Besides, who really trusts the computer to store their life's work? Explorer can show you everything if ask it to. To see where the files are, their names and extensions, and the hierarchy in which they reside, open Explorer and . . . explore.

Windows Explorer contains the following items:

Icon	Description
	Represents your desktop. If you click the Desktop icon, Windows 2000 Professional Explorer uses the file pane to show everything on your desktop — including any shortcut icons.
	Represents your computer, including its disks, printers, and any System Folders for fonts and Control Panel settings.
	Represents a hard drive. If you click the hard drive icon, Windows 2000 Professional Explorer displays folders and files on the hard drive.
	Represents a folder. If the folder is selected, it appears open. Otherwise, the folder appears closed. If the folder has subfolders within it, Windows 2000 Professional Explorer places a plus sign (+) in front of the folder.
	Represents a CD-ROM drive. If you click a CD, Explorer shows the files and folders located on that CD.
	Represents your computer's fonts. If you click the Fonts folder, Explorer shows all the fonts installed on your computer.
	Represents the Control Panel. If you click the Control Panel folder, Explorer shows the Control Panel applets used to alter and maintain your computer's settings.
	Represents the printers available to your computer. If you click the Printers folder, Explorer shows the printers connected to your computer or available over the network.

Icon	Description
	Represents the network your computer is attached to. If you click the Network Neighborhood folder, Explorer shows the computers, and their respective folders and files, connected to your network.
	Represents the Recycle Bin. If you click the Recycle Bin folder, Explorer shows the files and folders you have erased.
	Represents another computer that you can access remotely. If you click the Networking and Dial-Up Connections icon, the computer sets itself up for remote access.

Part III

Working with Programs

Programs and files are the lifeblood of your computer system. You must have a program to give your computer instructions. Whether you're word-processing, number-crunching, drawing, or sending e-mail, you work with a program to do these tasks.

In this part . . .

- ✓ Adding program shortcuts
- ✓ Adding programs to your system
- ✓ Starting and quitting programs
- ✓ Removing unwanted programs

Adding a Shortcut on the Desktop

Items that live as shortcuts on your Windows 2000 desktop are easy to put your hands on, just like the papers that live on top of your ordinary desk.

To put a shortcut on the Desktop:

1. Choose Start⇨Programs⇨Accessories⇨Windows Explorer.

2. Click the item, such as a file, program, folder, printer, or computer, for which you want to create a shortcut.

3. Choose File⇨Create Shortcut. Windows 2000 creates a shortcut designated by an icon with an arrow on it.

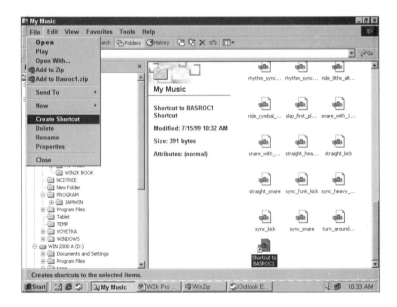

4. Drag the shortcut icon from Windows Explorer onto the desktop.

 You can also drag the item to the desktop with the right mouse button and then choose Create Shortcut(s) Here.

 Don't worry — when you delete a shortcut, the original item still exists on the disk.

Adding Programs to the Start Menu or Programs Menu

The Start and Programs menus make convenient access points for starting programs. Many programs automatically add their shortcuts to these menus when you install the program. For those programs that don't create a shortcut, you can add the shortcut yourself.

To add a shortcut to the Start menu or a submenu:

1. Click Start⇨Settings⇨Taskbar & Start Menu.

2. Click the Advanced options tab.

3. Click Add, and then follow the instructions in the Create Shortcut wizard.

You can also right-click an empty area on the taskbar and then click Properties to open the Taskbar Properties dialog box.

Adding Programs to Your System

Another application is always waiting in the wings to help you get your work done. Adding programs to your system is a simple process.

To add a program from a CD or floppy disk:

1. Click the Start button and choose Settings⇨Control Panel.

2. Click the Add/Remove Programs applet in the Control Panel.

3. Click Add New Programs and then click CD or Floppy.

4. Follow the instructions on your screen.

When using Add/Remove Programs, you can install only programs that were written for Windows operating systems.

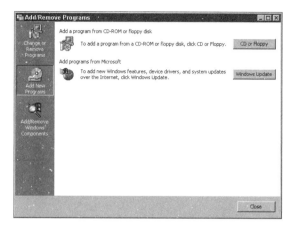

Clearing Documents from the Documents Menu

Windows 2000 automatically keeps track of the documents you've used during recent sessions and puts them close at hand on the Documents menu.

To clear the contents of the Documents menu:

1. Choose Start⇨Settings⇨Taskbar & Start Menu.

2. Click the Start Menu Options tab.

3. In the Customize Start menu, click Clear.

To open the Taskbar Properties dialog box, right-click an empty area on the taskbar and then click Properties.

Quitting an MS-DOS Program

To quit MS-DOS:

Type **exit** at the blinking cursor in the command-prompt window.

Quitting Programs

Getting out of a program is just as important as getting into one. To get out of a program, you have to give the program the instruction to quit or exit.

To quit a program, choose File⇨Exit.

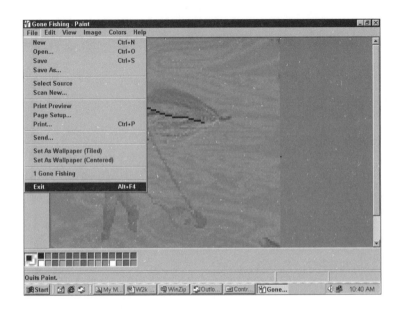

You can also quit a program by clicking the X in the box at the far right of the title bar.

Removing Program Shortcuts from the Start Menu

The Start menu can become cluttered with program shortcuts. Weed out those shortcuts when you find yourself having to sift through too many items to get to the program you want.

To remove a shortcut from the Start menu or a submenu:

1. Click Start⇨Settings⇨Taskbar & Start Menu.

2. Click the Start Menu Options tab, and then click Remove.

3. Click the item you want to remove, and then click Remove.

To open the Taskbar Properties dialog box, right-click an empty area on the taskbar and then click Properties.

When you remove a program shortcut, the original program remains on your computer.

Removing Programs from Your System

Keep your computer lean and mean by getting rid of programs that you use infrequently or don't use at all.

To remove programs from your system:

1. Click the Start button and then choose Settings⊃Control Panel.

2. Click the Add/Remove Programs applet in Control Panel.

3. Click Add New Programs, and then click CD or Floppy.

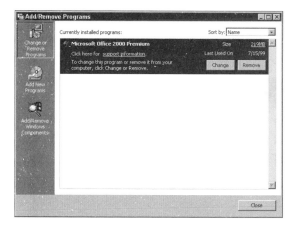

4. Follow the instructions on your screen.

TIP

When using Add/Remove Programs, you can install only programs that were written for Windows operating systems.

Starting an MS-DOS Program

Despite the fact that it seems like a Windows world these days, you may still need to run a DOS program or two.

To start an MS-DOS program from a command-prompt window, choose Start⇨Programs⇨Accessories and then click the Command Prompt icon.

To switch between a full screen and a window, press Alt+Enter.

Starting Programs by Using the Run Command

Some programs don't appear as icons on your desktop or shortcuts on your Start menu. These may be programs that you run infrequently, so you don't need to clutter up your Start or Programs menus with them. If this is the case, you can use the Run command to start the program.

To start a program by using the Run command:

1. Choose Start⇨Run.

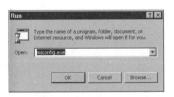

2. Type the path to the item you want to open in the Open box, or click Browse to locate it by using a My Computer – type window.

The drop-down list in the Open box lists items you have opened recently. Click an item in the list and then click OK to open it.

You can open a file or folder or connect to a shared computer by typing its path in the Open box. You can also connect to an Internet or intranet site; for example, to reach the Microsoft Web site, type **www.microsoft.com** in the Open box.

Starting Programs by Using the Start Button

Getting down to business means doing some actual work on your computer, which means you'll have to run a program or two.

To start a program:

1. Click Start⇨Programs.

2. Click the name of the program you want to start.

After you start a program, a button representing the program appears on the taskbar. To switch from one running program to another, click its taskbar button.

If a program you want doesn't appear on the Programs menu or one of its submenus, you can

1. Use Search to find it.

2. Right-click on the item and then choose Create Shortcut from the pop-up menu.

3. Drag the shortcut to the Start or Programs menu.

Starting Programs Each Time Windows 2000 Starts

You can have Windows 2000 start a program automatically each time you start or restart your computer.

To start a program each time you start Windows 2000:

1. Choose Start⇨Settings⇨Taskbar & Start Menu.

2. Click the Start Menu Options tab, and then click Advanced.

3. In the Start Menu folder, find the shortcut to the program you want to start each time you start Windows 2000 and drag it to the Startup folder.

To open the Taskbar Properties dialog box, right-click an empty area on the taskbar and then click Properties.

To add a program shortcut to the Startup menu, drag the icon to the Start button and then to the Programs menu and then drop it in the Startup menu.

Switching between Programs

As soon as you start working really hard, you may notice that it takes more than one program to get you through the day. You're running your word processor, a spreadsheet, and maybe a database, and your e-mail program is trolling for mail.

To switch between running programs, click a program's button on the taskbar.

 If you can't see the taskbar, you may have the Auto hide feature turned on. To redisplay the taskbar, point to the area of your screen where the taskbar is located.

You can also

◆ Switch to the next open program or document by pressing Alt+Tab.

◆ Cycle through open windows by holding down the Alt key and repeatedly pressing Tab.

Part IV

Using All Those Accessories

Included with Windows 2000 is an array of accessories, utilities, and games. Many of these accessories are mirror images of applications found in Windows 95 and Windows 98, but some are new for Windows 2000.

In this part . . .

- ✔ Using Calculator
- ✔ Playing CDs and videos
- ✔ Recording and playing back audio with Sound Recorder
- ✔ Playing games
- ✔ Using HyperTerminal
- ✔ Taking notes with Notepad
- ✔ Using Paint
- ✔ Working with WordPad

About the Accessories

When you choose Programs⇨Accessories from the Start menu, you see a whole slew of programs hiding on the Accessories menu, sometimes within other folders.

What It Is	Where It Is	What It Does
HyperTerminal	Start menu⇨Programs⇨ Accessories⇨HyperTerminal	A 32-bit modem-communications application (identical to the Windows 95/98 HyperTerminal application) hiding in its own folder.
Imaging	Start menu⇨Programs⇨ Accessories	Excellent graphics-viewing utility for Windows 2000 applications; has basic editing features and direct support for image acquisition from TWAIN-compliant scanners.
CD Player	Start menu⇨Programs⇨ Accessories⇨Multimedia	Accessory that enables you to play music CDs in your system's CD-ROM drive.
3D Pinball	Start menu⇨Programs⇨ Accessories⇨Games⇨ Windows 2000 CD-ROM	Cool 3-dimensional Pinball game, shows off the ActiveX capabilities of Windows 2000. (Can be addictive!)
WordPad	Start menu⇨Programs⇨ Accessories	A 32-bit text editor that replaces the Write application provided with earlier versions of Windows. WordPad utilizes common dialog boxes for opening, saving, and printing files; long filenames are easy to enter. Although not a full-blown word processor, WordPad makes simple documents and memos easy to create; it also accommodates text files too big for Notepad.
Paint	Start menu⇨Programs⇨ Accessories	A 32-bit graphics application that can read PCX and BMP files, and can write BMP files. As an OLE server application, Paint enables you to create information objects that can be linked to other documents or embedded in them. Paint is also MAPI-enabled, so it is easily integrated with Microsoft Exchange for sending images in e-mail or fax messages.

What It Is	*Where It Is*	*What It Does*
Calculator	Start menu⇨Programs⇨ Accessories	An on-screen mathematical and scientific calculator you can operate from your keypad (if you press Num Lock first).
Character Map	Start menu⇨Programs⇨ Accessories	A utility that shows you the complete character set for a particular font and enables you to copy characters to the Clipboard to paste into a document. If you need special characters that don't appear on your keyboard, find them quickly here.
Notepad	Start menu⇨Programs⇨ Accessories	A text editor for editing files or storing small amounts of information.
Media Player	Start menu⇨Programs⇨ Accessories⇨Multimedia	Enables you to play sound or video files.
Sound Recorder	Start menu⇨Programs⇨ Accessories⇨Multimedia	Enables you to record and play back sound.
Minesweeper	Start menu⇨Programs⇨ Accessories⇨Games	A cool game: Find the mines in the quickest time before they go kaboom.
Freecell	Start menu⇨Programs⇨ Accessories⇨Games	Just like the card game, except it builds your mouse skills.
Solitaire	Start menu⇨Programs⇨ Accessories⇨Games	Just like the card game; if you get caught playing it, you can always say you're testing your drag-and-drop skills.

If you don't see one or all of these utilities on your system, you may not have installed them during Windows 2000 Setup. To install the utilities, click the Add/Remove Programs applet in the Control Panel, click the Windows 2000 Setup tab, and then put check marks in the boxes next to those items you want to install.

Calculator

Do you have numbers to crunch, and you can't remember where you put your calculator? Windows 2000 offers several calculator functions built right in.

If you're not sure how you can use the Windows calculator functions to balance your checkbook or figure a loan payment, pick up a copy of *Everyday Math For Dummies,* by Charles Seiter, Ph.D.

To start Calculator:

1. Click the Start button.

The Start menu appears.

2. Point to Programs.

The Programs menu appears

3. Point to Accessories.

The Accessories menu appears.

4. Click Calculator to start the program.

To use your numeric keypad to enter numbers and operators, press the Num Lock key.

Quick basic math with Calculator

To perform a simple calculation:

1. Enter the first number in the calculation.

2. Click the appropriate button on the calculator for the operation you want

- + *(plus sign)* button to add
- – *(minus sign)* button to subtract
- * *(asterisk)* button to multiply
- / *(slash sign)* button to divide

3. Enter the next number of the calculation.

4. Enter any remaining operators and numbers.

5. Click the = (equal sign) button.

To perform a statistical calculation:

1. Choose View⇨Scientific.

2. Enter the first number.

3. Click the Sta button to display the Statistics Box.

   This step activates the Ave, Sum, s, and Dat buttons.

4. Click the Dat button.

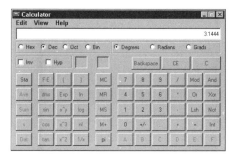

5. Do the following for each remaining data item:

   • Enter the data.

   • Click Dat.

   The new data appears in the Statistics Box each time you click the Dat button.

6. After you've entered all the data , click the RET button in the Statistics Box to return to Calculator.

7. Click the button for the statistics function you want to use:

   • *Ave* calculates the mean of the values.

   • *Sum* totals the values.

   • *s* calculates standard deviation.

Scientific number-crunching with Calculator

To perform a scientific calculation:

1. Choose View⇨Scientific.

   The 58-key version of Calculator appears.

2. Click the option button corresponding to the number system you desire:

- *decimal* (base 10)
- *hexadecimal* (base 16)
- *octal* (base 8)
- *binary* (base 2)

3. Do the following for each number in the calculation:

- Enter the first number.
- Click an operator.

4. Click the = (equal sign) button.

To convert a value to another number system:

1. Choose View⇨Scientific.

The 58-key version of Calculator appears.

2. Enter the number.

3. Click the option button corresponding to the number system to which you want to convert (decimal, hexadecimal, octal, or binary).

4. Click the unit of measurement in which to display the result.

CD Player

With CD Player, you can play an audio CD in your computer's CD-ROM or DVD drive.

To start the CD Player:

1. Click the Start button.

The Start menu appears.

2. Point to Programs.

The Programs menu appears.

3. Point to Accessories.

The Accessories menu appears.

4. Point to Multimedia.

5. Click CD Player.

CD Player looks much like an actual CD Player, providing buttons that enable you to play, stop, pause, skip a track, and advance or move back through a track. The following table lists other playback choices on the Options menu.

Option	Description
Random Order	Plays tracks on the CD in a nonsequential order.
Continuous Play	Plays the CD over again until you stop it.
Intro Play	Plays the beginning few seconds of each track.

Character Map

If your documents need stuff you won't find on most keyboards, you can use Windows 2000 Character Map to insert extended characters, happy faces, fancy Xs and Os, and other symbols.

To start the Character Map:

1. Click the Start button.

The Start menu appears.

2. Point to Programs.

The Programs menu appears.

3. Point to Accessories.

The Accessories menu appears.

4. Click Character Map to start the program.

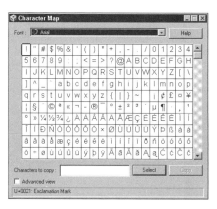

To insert a character into a document:

1. Position the cursor where you want to insert the character in the document.

2. In the Unicode Character Map dialog box, click the arrow next to the Font list box to view the drop-down list of available fonts. The character set changes to display the characters in the selected font.

3. Select a font.

4. Point to a character and then press and hold down the mouse button to see an enlarged picture of the character.

You can also press the Tab key until the cursor is in the character-selection area, and then use the arrow keys to see an enlarged picture of the character.

5. Double-click the character or click Select.

The selected character appears in the Characters to Copy box.

6. Select as many characters as you want to copy.

7. To put the characters showing in the Characters to Copy box on the Clipboard, click the Copy button.

8. Switch to the document into which you want to insert the characters.

9. Select the same font that you selected in the Unicode Character Map dialog box.

10. Position the cursor where you want the characters to appear.

11. Choose Edit➪Paste.

When you paste characters into some programs, they may lose the font you selected in the Unicode Character Map dialog box. To change the characters to the font you want, select them and apply the font you want (often by using Format➪Font or a similar command).

Games You Can Play

Windows 2000 doesn't just do work — it can play games, too. When you install Windows 2000 it automatically installs the following games:

✦ Freecell

✦ Minesweeper

✦ Pinball

✦ Solitaire

To start a game:

1. Click the Start button.

The Start menu appears.

2. Point to Programs.

The Programs menu appears.

3. Point to Accessories.

The Accessories menu appears.

4. Point to Games.

5. Click a game to start it.

HyperTerminal

You can use HyperTerminal and a modem to connect to a remote computer, even if it isn't running Windows. You can also use HyperTerminal to send and receive files or connect to computer bulletin boards and other information programs.

Starting HyperTerminal

To start HyperTerminal:

1. Click the Start button.

The Start menu appears.

2. Point to Programs.

The Programs menu appears.

3. Point to Accessories.

The Accessories menu appears.

4. Click HyperTerminal or one of the existing connections.

The HyperTerminal Window opens.

Setting up a new connection

To set up a new connection:

1. Choose File⇨New Connection.

2. Type a name that describes the connection and click an appropriate icon. Then click the OK button.

3. Enter the information for the call and then click the OK button.

4. To dial the call, click the Dial button.

Calling a remote computer

To call a remote computer:

1. Choose File⇨Open and then double-click the connection you want to use.

2. Choose Call⇨Connect.

3. Click the Dial button.

Sending a file to a remote computer

To send a file to a remote computer:

1. Make sure that the computer you're calling has the necessary file transfer to receive the file. Call the remote computer.

2. Choose Transfer⇨Send File.

The Send File dialog box appears.

3. In the Filename box, type the path and name of the file. Or click the Browse button to display the Select File to Send dialog box.

To change the protocol you use to send the file, use the Protocol list box to select it.

4. To send the file, click the Send button.

If you want to send a standard text file to the remote computer, choose Transfer⇨Send Text File (instead of Transfer⇨Send File as described in Step 2).

Receiving a file from a remote computer

To receive a file from a remote computer:

1. Call the remote computer using the steps in the section Calling a remote computer.

2. Have the user at the remote computer use the software on the remote computer to send (download) the file to your computer.

3. On your computer, choose Transfer⟿Receive File.

The Receive File dialog box appears.

4. Type the path to the folder in which you want to store the file. Or click the Browse button to display the Select a Folder dialog box and then select the folder in which you want to place the file.

5. In the Use Receiving Protocol list box, click the protocol you want the remote computer to use when it sends your file.

Changing port settings

The original port settings for your modem are usually correct when your modem is installed. For special requirements, however, you may need to modify the port settings.

To change the port settings for a particular modem connection:

1. Click the Start button.

The Start menu appears.

2. Point to Programs.

The Programs menu appears.

3. Point to Accessories.

The Accessories menu appears.

4. Click the HyperTerminal that you want to change.

5. Choose File⟿Properties to display the Properties dialog box for that connection.

6. Click the Connect To tab.

7. Click the Configure button to display the Properties dialog box for that modem.

8. Click the Connection tab and then make the changes you need.

9. To change settings such as flow control and error correction, click the Advanced button and then make the changes you need.

Saving a HyperTerminal session

To save a HyperTerminal session to a file:

1. Choose Transfer⟿Capture Text.

The Capture Text dialog box appears.

2. Type a name that describes the file the text will be saved in.

3. Click the Start button.

To stop saving a HyperTerminal session to a file:

1. Choose Transfer⇨Capture Text.

2. Click Pause or Stop.

 You can also send the session text directly to a printer by choosing Transfer⇨Capture to Printer. When you end the call, the text is sent to your default printer.

Media Player

Media Player enables you to play different types of media files, such as music from a CD, audio from a sound file, or video from a video file.

The Media Player is intuitive to use because its buttons represent the buttons of a tape recorder.

Starting Media Player

To start Media Player:

1. Click the Start button.

The Start menu appears.

2. Point to Programs.

The Programs menu appears.

3. Point to Accessories.

The Accessories menu appears.

4. Point to Multimedia.

5. Click Media Player to start the program.

Opening and Playing a Media File

To open and play a file:

1. From Media Player, choose File⇨Open.

The Open dialog box appears.

2. Use the Open dialog box to select the directory containing the media file and then select the file.

3. Click the Open button.

The file loads into Media Player.

4. Click the Play button to play the Media file.

To stop playing the media file, click the Stop button.

Notepad

You can use Notepad to create or edit *unformatted* ASCII (text-only) files that are smaller than 64K, about 60,000 characters.

Starting Notepad

To start Notepad:

1. Click the Start button.

The Start menu appears.

2. Point to Programs.

The Programs menu appears.

3. Point to Accessories.

The Accessories menu appears.

4. Click Notepad to start the program.

Keeping a log

You may be the type who likes to keep a journal of daily activities. If so, Notepad is a nifty tool for tracking your time, thoughts, and/or events of the day.

To keep a log by using Notepad:

1. On the first line of a Notepad document, type **.LOG** at the left margin, making sure that you include the period.

2. Save the document.

Every time you open this file, Notepad appends the current time and date to the end of the file.

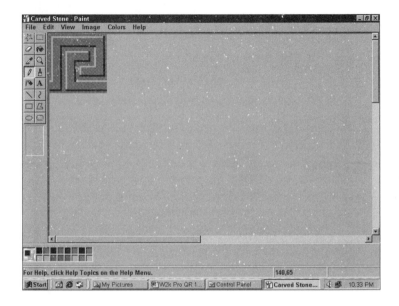

Paint

You can create, edit, or view pictures by using Paint. You can paste a Paint picture into another document you create or use it as your desktop background. You can even use Paint to view and edit scanned photos.

Starting Paint

To start Paint:

1. Click the Start button. The Start menu appears.

2. Point to Programs. The Programs menu appears.

3. Point to Accessories.

The Accessories menu appears.

4. Click Paint to start the program.

Opening a file

To open a file:

1. Choose File⇨Open to display the Open dialog box.

2. In the Look In box, select the drive that contains the file you want to open.

3. Below the Look In box, select the folder that contains the file you want to open.

4. Select the file's name or type it in the File Name box. Then click the Open button to display the file.

Using a picture as the desktop background

To cover the screen with *repetitions* of your picture, choose File⇨Set As Wallpaper (Tiled).

To put your bitmap in the *center* of your screen, choose File⇨Set As Wallpaper (Centered).

You must *save* a picture before you can use it as wallpaper.

Printing a picture

To print a picture, choose File⇨Print.

To see how the printed picture will look before you print, choose File⇨Print Preview.

Setting margins and changing orientation

To set margins, change printing orientation, or set paper size, choose File⇨Page Setup and then choose the appropriate tab from the dialog box.

Sound Recorder

Sound Recorder enables you to record and play back audio. You can, for example, record your voice, save the recording in a file, and give the file to someone else, who then can play back the file.

To use Sound Recorder, your computer must be equipped with a sound card, a microphone, and a pair of speakers.

Starting Sound Recorder

To start Sound Recorder:

1. Click the Start button.

The Start menu appears.

2. Point to Programs.

The Programs menu appears.

3. Point to Accessories.

The Accessories menu appears.

4. Point to Multimedia.

5. Click Sound Recorder to start the program.

Opening and playing a sound file

To open and play a file:

1. From Sound Recorder, choose File⇨Open.

The Open dialog box appears.

2. Use the Open dialog box to select the directory containing the sound file and then select the file.

3. Click the Open button.

The file loads into Media Player.

4. Click the Play button to play the Media file.

Recording and saving a sound

To record and save a sound:

1. Start Sound Recorder.

Before you start recording, make sure your microphone is plugged in.

2. Click the Record button.

You are now recording what the microphone picks up. When finished, click the Stop button.

3. Choose File⇨Save As.

The Save As dialog box opens.

4. Select the directory in which to save the file and then type the name of the file in the File Name text box.

5. Click Save.

Now that you have saved the sound, you can open it and play it back. You also can copy the sound file or e-mail it to someone else.

Altering a sound file

You can do interesting things to the sound that you record with Sound Recorder. For example, you can mix the sound recording with another sound file, or you can add echo to a recording. The following table describes the ways you can alter a sound file.

Menu	Alteration	Description
Edit	Insert File	Enables you to insert another sound into the current sound file, combining the two files.
Edit	Mix with File	Enables you to mix two sounds together so that you hear both at the same time when played.
Effects	Increase Volume (by 25%)	Enables you to make a sound louder.
Effects	Decrease Volume	Enables you to make a sound softer.
Effects	Increase Speed (by 100%)	Makes a sound play twice as fast.
Effects	Decrease Speed	Enables you to slow down a sound.
Effects	Add Echo	Enables you to add an echoing effect to the sound.
Effects	Reverse	Enables you to play a sound backward.

Before you start altering a sound, saving the original sound is a good idea. Saving your modified versions of the sound in different files (with different filenames) is also a good idea — you can revert back to an earlier modified version or to the original sound. When you have a modified sound you like, delete the other versions (except for the original); unused sound files just sit there taking up disk space.

Volume Control

If you have a sound card in your computer, you can use Volume Control to turn the sound up or down, whether it comes from your computer's speakers, microphone, or CD-ROM drive.

Starting Volume Control

To start the Volume Control program:

1. Click the Start button.

   The Start menu appears.

2. Point to Programs.

   The Programs menu appears.

3. Point to Accessories on the Programs menu.

   The Accessories menu appears.

4. Point to Multimedia on the Accessories menu.

5. Click Volume Control to start the program.

Adjusting playback volume

To adjust the playback volume, drag the Volume Control slider up to raise the volume or down to lower the volume. To change the balance between the left and right speakers, drag the Balance slider to the left or right.

If your computer has more than one device (for example, a MIDI or .WAV device), you can set the volume for each device.

To turn off the sound, click the Mute All check box in the Volume Control dialog box so that a check mark appears.

Adjusting recording volume

To adjust the recording volume:

1. Choose Options⇔Properties to display the Properties dialog box.

2. Click the Recording radio button.

3. Make sure that the device you want to adjust the volume for is checked — and then click the OK button.

4. Drag the Volume Control slider up to raise the volume or down to lower the volume.

Adjusting voice-input volume

To adjust the voice-input volume when recording a voice:

1. Choose Options⇔Properties and then click the Other option button in the Properties dialog box.

2. Select Voice Commands from the drop-down list box.

3. Make sure that the device for which you want to adjust the volume is checked — and then click the OK button.

4. Drag the Volume Control slider up to raise the volume or down to lower the volume.

To change the balance between the left and right speakers, drag the Balance slider to the left or right.

WordPad

Besides acting as a text editor for big text files, WordPad functions as a word processor for short documents. You can format a document in WordPad with various font and paragraph styles.

Because WordPad comes with Windows 2000 and is relatively modest about its use of computer resources, it's ideal to use as a word processor on your notebook computer. You can open it later in Word or another word processor.

Starting WordPad

To start WordPad:

1. Click the Start button.

The Start menu appears.

2. Point to Programs.

The Programs menu appears.

3. Point to Accessories on the Programs menu.

The Accessories menu appears.

4. Click WordPad to start the program.

Creating a new document

To create a new document:

1. Choose File⇨New to display the New dialog box.

2. Click the file type you want to create and then begin typing.

You can choose Word, Rich Text, or unformatted text.

To name a new file, choose File⇨Save As.

Saving changes

To save changes to a document, choose File⇨Save.

To save an existing document with a new name, click File⇨Save As and then type a new name in the File Name box.

Opening a document

To open a document:

1. Choose File⇨Open to display the Open dialog box.

2. In the Look In list box, select the drive that contains the document you want to open.

3. Below the Look In box, select the folder that contains the document you want to open.

4. Select the document's name or type it in the File Name box.

5. Click the Open button.

If you don't see what you're looking for, select a different file type or All Documents from the Files of Type list.

To open a document you opened recently, select its name from the bottom of the File menu.

Undoing an action

To undo your last action, choose Edit⇨Undo.

To undo a deletion, choose Edit⇨Undo.

Deleting text

To delete text:

1. Select the text you want to delete.

2. To remove text so that you can place it in another part of the document, choose Edit⇨Cut. To erase text entirely from the document, press the Delete key.

Selecting text

To select all the text in a document, choose Edit⇨Select All.

To cancel a selection, click anywhere in the document.

Searching for text

To search for text:

1. In the document, click where you want to start searching.

2. Choose Edit⇨Find to display the Find dialog box.

3. Enter the search text in the Find what box.

4. To find additional instances of the same text, click the Find Next button.

Inserting date and time

To insert the current date and time:

1. Click where you want the date and time to appear.

2. Choose Insert⇨Date and Time to display the Date and Time dialog box.

3. Select the format you want for the date or the time.

Changing text wrap

Can't see all your text? To change the way text wraps on your screen:

1. Choose View⇨Options to display the Options dialog box.

2. In the Word wrap box, select the wrapping option you want and then click OK.

After you turn on a Word wrap option, what you see is not what you get when you print the document. The Word wrapping options only affect how text appears on your screen. The printed document reflects the margin settings specified in the Page Setup dialog box.

Inserting bullets

Do you need to present alternatives or emphasize several different aspects of a topic? Use bullet points.

To create a bulleted list:

1. Click where you want the bullet list to start.

2. Choose Format⇨Bullet Style and then enter text. When you press Enter, another bullet is displayed on the next line.

3. To end the bullet list, choose Format⇨Bullet Style again.

Changing fonts

If you want to add flair, change the font. Make words stand out with bold typeface, call attention to a phrase with italics, or make a statement more like a headline by enlarging it to 24-point type.

As a rule, don't use more than three fonts in the same document.

To change a font type, style, and size:

1. Select the text you want to format.

2. Choose Format⇨Font.

3. Select the options you want.

You can specify the font for new text by changing the font settings before you begin to type. To change the font for an entire document, choose Edit⇨Select All before choosing the Format menu.

Previewing your document

Do you want a preview of how your document will look in hard copy before you print it?

To see how the document will look in print:

1. Choose File⇨Print Preview.

2. To return to the previous view from Print Preview, click the Close button.

Part V

Working the Web with Internet Explorer 5

To search and view information on the World Wide Web, all you need is an Internet connection and Internet Explorer.

In this part . . .

✓ Saving Web pages

✓ Sending Web pages as e-mail

✓ Bookmarking Web pages

✓ Searching the Web

Adding a Web Page to Your Links Bar

The Links bar lives right next to the Address bar and is a convenient place to add links to a few Web pages that you use frequently. *Links* are pointers to Web pages and provide a quick and direct route to a Web site. Just click the link to display the page.

You can add a page to the Links bar in a variety of ways:

✦ Drag the icon for the page from your *Address bar* to your Links bar.

✦ Drag a link from a *Web page* to your Links bar.

✦ Drag a link to the *Links folder* in your Favorites list.

If the Links bar does not appear on the toolbar, here's how to get it:

1. Click the View menu.

2. Point to Toolbars.

3. Click Links.

 If you forget to add Web pages to your Favorites or Links bar, click the History button on the toolbar. The History list shows where you've been — today, yesterday, or a few weeks ago. Click a name from the list to display the page.

Bookmarking a Web Page

When you find Web sites or pages that you like, you can bookmark them — add them to your list of favorite pages to keep track of them. Any time you want to open a page, just click the Favorites button on the toolbar, and then click the shortcut in the Favorites list.

To add a Web page to your list of favorites:

1. Enter the Web page address (URL) to go to the page you want to add to your Favorites list.

2. On the Favorites menu, click Add to Favorites.

3. Type a new name for the page if you want.

Browsing Web Pages Offline

When you make a Web page available offline, you can read its content when your computer is not connected to the Internet.

1. On the Favorites menu, click Add to Favorites.

2. Select the Make available offline check box.

3. To specify a schedule for updating that page, and how much content to download, click Customize and follow the instructions on your screen.

Before you go offline, make sure that you have the latest version of your pages:

1. Click the Tools menu.

2. Click Synchronize.

If you just want to view a Web page offline, and you don't need to update the content, you can save the page on your computer. See "Saving a Web Page," in this part.

To make an existing favorite item available offline:

1. On the Favorites menu, click Organize Favorites.

2. Click the page you want to make available offline.

3. Select the Make Available Offline check box.

To specify a schedule for updating that page and how much content to download, click Properties.

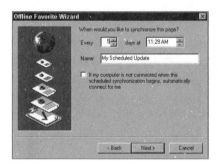

Changing Fonts and Background Colors

When Web authors and designers create Web pages, they often specify particular font colors and sizes, typefaces, and background colors. You can override any or all of these settings, which is useful if you have a visual impairment and need sharper contrast to make text more legible.

To change page colors:

1. Click Internet Options on the Tools menu in Internet Explorer.

2. On the General tab, click Colors.

3. Change the settings as desired.

To display text in a different font:

1. Click Internet Options on the Tools menu in Internet Explorer.

2. On the General tab, click Fonts.

3. In the lists for Web page font and Plain text font, click the fonts you want.

To display text larger or smaller:

1. Click Text Size on the View menu.

2. Click the point size you want to apply to the text.

Changing the Toolbar

To change the appearance of the toolbar:

✦ You can add or remove standard toolbar buttons, use smaller buttons, and/or change the order in which they appear on the toolbar. Just right-click the toolbar and then click Customize.

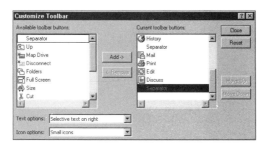

✦ You can move or resize the Address bar, Links bar, and radio bar by dragging them up, down, left, or right.

✦ You can hide the Address bar, Links bar, or radio bar by right-clicking the toolbar and then clicking to clear the check mark for each item you want to hide.

✦ You can add items to the Links bar by dragging the icon from the Address bar (or dragging a link from a Web page) and dropping it on the Links bar.

✦ You can rearrange items on the Links bar by dragging them to a new location on the bar.

The radio toolbar is available in Internet Explorer when you install Windows Media Player.

Choosing Your Home Page

Your home page is the page displayed every time you open Internet Explorer. Make sure that it's a page you want to view frequently, or make it easy to customize so that you can get quick access to all the information you want.

To change your home page:

1. Go to the page you want to appear when you first start Internet Explorer.

2. On the Tools menu, click Internet Options.

3. Click the General tab.

4. In the Home page area, click Use Current.

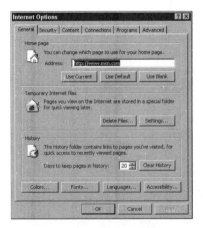

To restore your original home page, click Use Default.

Copying Information from a Web Page

The Web holds a vast amount of information. You're bound to want to copy some portion of it.

1. Select the information you want to copy.

2. Click the Edit menu.

3. Click Copy.

Creating a Shortcut to a Web Page

When you find a site that you want to pop into and out of frequently, just create a shortcut: Right-click in the page and then click Create Shortcut.

Displaying Web Pages Faster

Sometimes the Web just doesn't seem fast enough. Speed it up a bit by turning off graphics.

To turn off graphics and display all Web pages faster:

1. On the Tools menu in Internet Explorer, click Internet Options.

The Internet Options dialog box appears.

2. Click the Advanced tab.

3. Scroll down to the Multimedia area and clear one or more of the Show pictures, Play animations, Play videos, or Play sounds check boxes.

 If the Show pictures or Play videos check box is cleared, you can still display an individual picture or animation on a Web page by right-clicking its icon and then clicking Show Picture.

Finding What You Want on the Web

You can find information on the Web in a variety of ways.

✦ Click the Search button on the toolbar to gain access to a number of search providers. Type a word or phrase in the Search box and then press Enter.

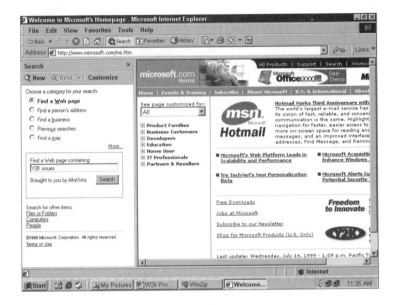

◆ Type **go**, **find**, or **?** followed by a word or phrase in the Address bar, and then press Enter. Internet Explorer starts a search using its predetermined search provider.

◆ After you go to a Web page, you can search for specific text on that page by clicking the Edit menu and then clicking Find (on the same page).

If a Web address doesn't work, Internet Explorer asks whether you want to search for similar Web addresses. You can change this setting so that Internet Explorer searches automatically without prompting.

Printing a Web Page

To print a Web page:

1. On the File menu, click Print.

2. Set the printing options you want.

To print a frame or item in a Web page, right-click the frame or item and then click Print or Print Frame.

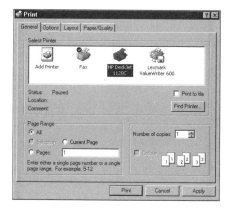

Saving a Web Page

To save a Web page on your computer:

1. On the File menu, click Save As.

2. Double-click the folder you want to save the page in.

3. In the File Name box, type a name for the page.

4. In the Save as Type box, select a file type.

- To save all the files needed to display this page in their original formats (including graphics, frames, and style sheets), click Web Page, Complete.

- To save all the information needed to display this page in a single MIME-encoded file, click Web Archive. This option saves a snapshot of the current Web page. (This option is available only if you have installed Outlook Express 5 or later.)

- To save just the current HTML page without the graphics, sounds, or other files, click Web Page, HTML Only.

- To save just the text from the current Web page in straight text format, click Text Only.

 With the Web Page, Complete and Web Archive saving options, you can view all of a Web page offline (without adding the page to your Favorites list) and mark it for offline viewing.

Sending a Web Page in E-Mail

While scouring the Web, you might come across a Web page that you want to share. Send the entire page or the link as e-mail.

Click the File menu, point to Send, and then click Page by E-mail or Link by E-mail. Complete the mail message window and then send the message.

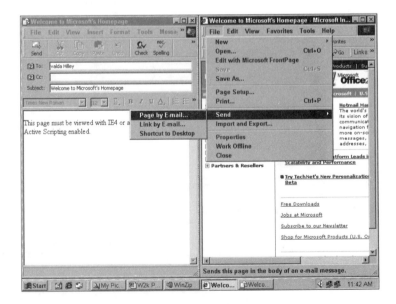

You must have an e-mail account and an e-mail program set up on your computer.

Using a Web Page as Desktop Wallpaper

Found a Web page that you just must have? Keep a snapshot of it on your desktop.

Right-click the image on the Web page and then click Set as Wallpaper.

Viewing Web Pages Offline

After you mark your favorite pages for viewing offline, you can read them offline without running up online fees.

To view Web pages without being connected to the Internet:

1. Before you disconnect from the Internet, click the Tools menu and then click Synchronize.

2. When you're ready to work offline, click the File menu and then click Work Offline.

3. In your Favorites list, click the item you want to view.

If you choose to work offline, Internet Explorer will always start in Offline mode until you click Work Offline again to clear the check mark.

Part VI

Using Outlook Express E-Mail and News

All you need to exchange e-mail messages with anyone in Cyberspace is an Internet connection and Microsoft Outlook Express. You can also join any number of newsgroups and participate in discussions.

In this part . . .

🖙 **Creating and sending e-mail messages**

🖙 **Reading e-mail messages**

🖙 **Sending files in e-mail messages**

🖙 **Posting messages to newsgroups**

Adding a Mail or News Account

In order to send and receive e-mail or newsgroup messages, you need the following information from your Internet service provider (ISP) or local area network (LAN) administrator:

For mail accounts:

+ The type of mail server you use (POP3, IMAP, or HTTP)

+ Your account name and password

+ The name of the incoming mail server

+ The name of an outgoing mail server

For a news account:

+ The name of the news server you want to connect to

+ If required, your account name and password

When you have this information, you're ready to set up a mail or news account.

To add a mail account:

1. On the Tools menu, click Accounts. The Internet Accounts dialog box appears.

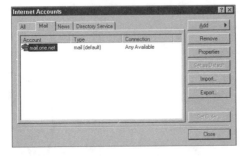

2. In the Internet Accounts dialog box, click the Add button.

3. Select Mail to open the Internet Connection Wizard.

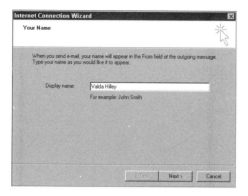

4. Enter your name in the Display Name box (located in the Your Name user interface box) and then click Next. The Internet E-mail Address screen appears.

5. If you already have an e-mail address, choose I Already Have an E-mail Address That I'd Like to Use.

6. Enter your e-mail address, if you have one, in the E-mail Address box and then click Next. The E-mail Server Names screen appears.

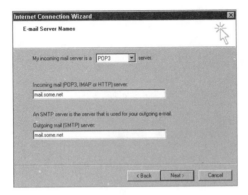

7. Select the type of mail server you will connect to from the My Incoming Mail Server Is a ____ Server list box.

8. Enter the address of your incoming mail server in the Incoming Mail (POP3, IMAP or HTTP) Server field.

9. Enter the address of your outgoing mail server in the Outgoing Mail (SMTP) Server field.

10. Click Next. The Internet Mail Logon screen appears.

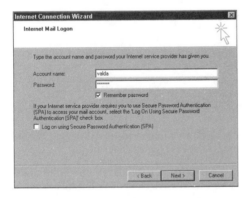

11. Enter your account name and password in the appropriate boxes.

12. Check the Remember Password box to have Outlook Express remember your password each time you log on.

13. Click Next to finish the process.

Adding Contacts from Outlook Express

When you receive e-mail, you can quickly add the sender's name and e-mail address to your address book with a click of your mouse.

To add contacts to your address book from Outlook Express:

1. Open the message by double-clicking on it.

2. Click Tools⇨Add Sender to Address Book.

 Outlook Express can automatically add to your Address Book the addresses of people whose messages you reply to. Click Tools⇨ Options⇨Send and then click Automatically Put People I Reply to in My Address Book.

Adding Contacts to Your Address Book

To add a contact to your address book:

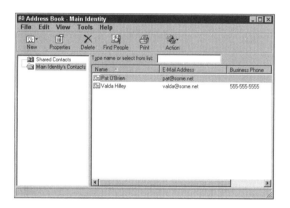

1. In the Address Book, select the folder to which you want to add a contact.

2. Click the New button on the toolbar and then click New Contact.

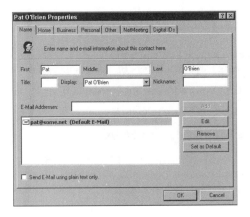

3. On the Name tab, type at least the First and Last names for the contact. The name automatically appears in the Display box.

4. Enter the contact's e-mail address if you want Outlook Express to automatically fill in the e-mail address when you compose an e-mail message to the contact.

5. On each of the other tabs, add any information you want.

Adding Folders

To add a folder:

1. Click File⇨Folder⇨New.

2. Type a name in the Folder Name text box.

3. Select a location for the new folder.

Assigning Importance to a Message

When you send a new message or reply to a message, you can assign the message a priority so that the recipient knows to either look at it right away (High Priority) or read it when time permits (Low Priority).

✦ A high-priority message has an exclamation point next to it.

✦ A low-priority message has a downward arrow next to it.

To change the priority of an outgoing mail message, do either of the following:

✦ In the New Message window, click the Priority button on the toolbar and then select the priority you want.

✦ Click the Message menu, choose Set Priority, and then select a priority option.

Checking Spelling in a Message

To check the spelling in messages, open the New Message window and do one of the following:

✦ Click the Spelling button on the toolbar.

✦ Choose Tools⇨Spelling.

 Outlook Express uses the spell-checker that installs with Microsoft Word, Microsoft Excel, and Microsoft PowerPoint 95/97. Spell-checking is not available unless you have one of these programs installed.

 You can customize the way your spell-checker works. Click Tools⇨Options and select the Spelling tab.

Copying Messages

To copy a message to another folder:

1. In the source folder's message list, select the message you want to copy.

2. Choose Edit⇨Copy to Folder and select a destination folder.

 You can also copy a message by selecting it in the source folder's message list and holding down the Ctrl key while you drag it to a new folder.

Creating a Business Card

A business card is your contact information from the Address Book in vCard format, which can be used with a wide variety of digital devices and operating systems.

To create a business card:

1. In the Address Book, create an entry for yourself and then select your name from the Address Book list.

2. Choose File⇨Export⇨Business Card (vCard).

3. Select a location in which to store the file, and then click Save.

You must have your contact information in the Address Book before you can create a business card.

See also "Adding Contacts to Your Address Book" in this part for more information.

To import a business card:

1. In the Address Book, choose File➪Import➪Business Card (vCard).

2. Locate the business card file on your computer or a network drive, select it, and then click Open.

To insert a business card in all messages:

1. Choose Tools➪Options➪Compose. The Options dialog box appears.

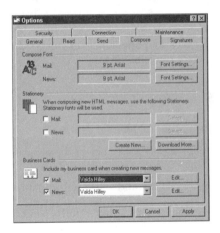

2. In the Business Cards section, select the Mail or News check boxes, and then select a business card from the drop-down list.

To add a business card or signature to an individual message:

In a message window, choose Insert➪My Business Card.

 To insert your business card, you must first create a contact in your Address Book for yourself.

 You can include the business card of any contact in your Address Book in a message.

Deleting a Mail Message

To delete a mail message:

1. In the message list, select the message.

2. Click the Delete button on the toolbar.

 To restore a deleted message, open the Deleted Items folder and then drag the message back to the Inbox or other folder.

Deleting Folders

To delete a folder:

1. Click the folder in the Folders list.

2. Choose File⇨Folder⇨Delete.

You cannot delete the Inbox, Outbox, Sent Items, Deleted Items, or Drafts folders.

Forwarding a Mail Message

To forward a mail message:

1. Select the message you want to forward.

2. Choose Message⇨Forward.

3. Enter the e-mail name for each recipient you want to forward the message to, separating each name with a comma or a semicolon.

4. Type your message and click the Send button on the toolbar.

Moving Messages

To move a message to another folder:

1. In the source folder's message list, select the message you want to move.

2. Choose Edit⇨Move to Folder and then select the destination folder.

 You can also move a message by selecting it in the source folder's message list and dragging it to a new folder.

Opening an Attachment

When a message has a file attached to it, a paper clip is displayed next to it in the message list.

To open a file attachment:

In the message window, click the paper-clip icon in the message header and then click the filename.

 At the top of the message window, you can also double-click the file attachment icon in the message header.

Opening the Address Book

To open the Address Book from Outlook Express, do one of the following:

✦ Click the Addresses button on the toolbar.

✦ Click Tools⇨Address Book.

✦ To open the Address Book from within a message window, click the To, Cc, or Bcc icon.

Posting Messages to Newsgroups

To post a message to a newsgroup:

1. In the Folders list, select the newsgroup you want to post a message to.

2. Click the New Post button on the toolbar.

3. Type a subject for your message in the Subject box. Outlook Express cannot post a message that does not contain a subject.

4. Compose your message and then click the Send button.

 You can send a given message to more than one newsgroup at a time only if all the newsgroups are on the same news server. To post a message to newsgroups on other news servers, create a separate message for each news server.

Printing a Message

You can print a message that is displayed in the preview pane or one that is open in a separate window.

To print a message, click File⇨Print and then select the print options you want.

Reading Mail Messages

After Outlook Express downloads your messages or after you click the Send/Recv button on the toolbar, you can read messages either in a separate window or in the preview pane.

To read your messages:

1. Click the Inbox icon on either the Outlook bar or the Folders list.

2. Select the message you want to read, as follows:

✦ To view the message in the preview pane, click the message in the message list.

✦ To view the message in a separate window, double-click the message in the message list.

Replying to a Mail Message

To reply to an e-mail message:

1. In the message list, click the message you want to reply to.

2. Click the Reply button on the toolbar.

3. Type your message and then click the Send button.

Replying to Newsgroup Messages

To reply to a newsgroup message:

1. In the message list, click the message you want to reply to.

2. Click the Reply button on the toolbar.

3. To reply to the whole newsgroup, click the Reply Group button on the toolbar.

4. Type your message and then click the Send button.

Saving a Copy of a Message

To save the message in your file system:

1. Click Save As from the File menu.

2. Select a format (mail, text, or HTML) and a location.

3. Click Save to save the message.

Saving a File Attachment

When a message has a file attached to it, a paper clip is displayed next to it in the message list.

To save a file attachment:

Click File⇨Save Attachments and then click the filename.

Sending a File in a Message

To insert a file in a message:

1. Click anywhere in the message window.

2. Choose Insert⇨File Attachment and then find the file you want to attach.

3. Select the file and click Attach. The file is listed in the Attach box in the message header.

TIP You can also add a text (*.txt) file to the body of your mail message by choosing Insert⇨Text from File.

Sending a Picture in a Message

To insert a picture in a message:

1. In the message, click where you want the image to appear.

2. Choose Insert⇨Picture, and then click the Browse button to find the image file.

3. Enter Layout and Spacing information for the image file as needed.

If you cannot select the Picture command, make sure that HTML formatting is turned on by choosing Format⇨Rich Text (HTML) in the message window. A black dot appears by the command when it is selected.

Sending E-Mail Messages

To send an e-mail message:

1. Click the New Mail button on the toolbar. The New Message window appears.

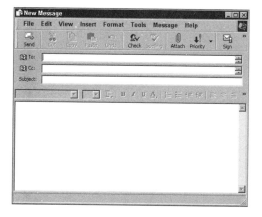

2. In the To and Cc boxes, type the e-mail name of each recipient, separating names with a comma or semicolon.

3. In the Subject box, type a message title.

4. Type your message and then click the Send button on the New Message toolbar.

 To add e-mail names from the Address Book, click the book icon in the New Message window next to To, Cc, and Bcc and then select names.

Sending Messages on Stationery

With Outlook Express stationery, you can really get attention by sending attractive messages for both e-mail and newsgroups. Stationery can include a background image, unique text-font colors, and custom margins.

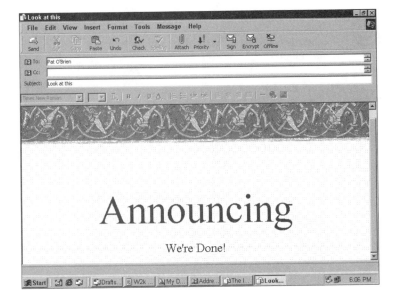

To apply stationery to all your outgoing messages:

1. Choose Tools⇨Options⇨Compose.

2. In the Stationery area, check the Mail or News check box.

3. Click Select to choose the stationery you want.

To apply stationery to an individual message:

> Choose Message⇨New Message Using and then select a stationery.

To apply or change stationery after you start a message:

> Choose Format⇨Apply Stationery and then select the stationery.

Part VII

Print(ing) or Perish

Computers are supposed to increase your productivity. And as your productivity increases, so does the amount of paper you use. To get all that productivity out of your computer, you have to print documents. In fact, the printed documents are proof that you really have put in a full day's work.

In this part . . .

- ✔ **Canceling the printing of a document**
- ✔ **Changing the number of copies to print**
- ✔ **Changing the paper size**
- ✔ **Changing the printing orientation**
- ✔ **Connecting a printer directly to your computer**
- ✔ **Printing a document**
- ✔ **Viewing a list of documents waiting to print**

Adding a Printer to Your Computer

Windows 2000 is smart enough to install most printers automatically. However, it may not fully recognize some older printers, and you may have to provide additional information or drivers to complete the installation.

Here's how to add a printer to your computer automatically:

1. Use a printer cable to connect the printer to the appropriate port (usually a parallel port, LPT port) on your computer. If you need help with this, check the manual that came with your printer.

2. Choose Start⇨Settings⇨Printers to open the Printers window.

3. Double-click Add Printer to start the Add Printer Wizard, and then click Next.

4. Click Local Printer, make sure that Automatically Detect My Printer is checked, and then click Next to start the Found New Hardware Wizard.

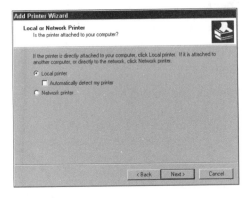

5. Follow the instructions on the screen to finish installing the printer. The printer icon appears in your Printers folder.

Alternatively, you can start or restart your computer, after connecting your printer, to allow Windows 2000 to start the Found New Hardware Wizard automatically.

If you install a Universal Serial Bus (USB) printer, Windows 2000 detects it and automatically starts the Found New Hardware Wizard. You don't need to shut down or restart your computer. Simply follow the instructions on the screen to finish installing the printer. (You don't need to continue with the instructions below.)

If you install an infrared printer, Windows 2000 detects it automatically and places an icon for the printer in the status area of the taskbar.

 WARNING

To add and set up a printer connected directly to your computer, you must log on as a member of the Administrators group. Part I, Getting to Know Windows 2000, explains how to log on as an Administrator.

Follow these steps to add a printer to your computer manually:

1. Choose Start➪Settings➪Printers to open the Printers window.

2. Double-click Add Printer to start the Add Printer Wizard, and then click Next.

3. Click Local Printer, uncheck the Automatically Detect My Printer check box, and then click Next to start the Found New Hardware Wizard. The Select the Printer Port dialog box appears.

4. Select the port to which your printer is attached and then click Next. The Add Printer Wizard dialog box appears.

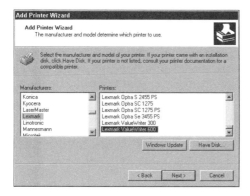

5. Select the printer's manufacturer and model and then click Next. The Name Your Printer dialog box appears.

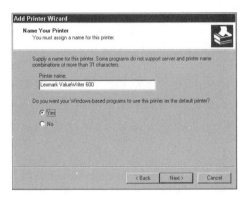

6. Enter a name for the printer in the Printer Name field.

7. Choose Yes or No to tell Windows whether you want this printer to be the default printer for your Windows-based programs. Odds are you do.

8. Click Next. The Printer Sharing dialog box appears.

9. Choose Do Not Share This Printer, the default setting, or Share As to indicate whether you want this printer to be accessible to others on your network.

See Part VIII for information on sharing printers.

10. Click Next. The Print Test Page dialog box appears.

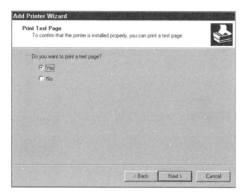

11. Choose Yes or No to indicate whether you want to print a test page at this time and then click Next. The Completing the Add Printer Wizard appears.

If you want to print a test page, make sure that your printer is turned on and ready to print before you begin the test.

12. Click Finish to complete the add printer process. The printer icon appears in your Printers folder.

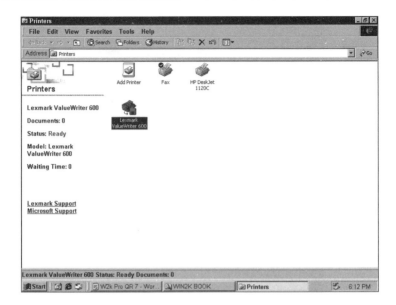

Canceling the Printing of a Document

To cancel the printing of a document, follow these steps:

1. Choose Start⇨Settings⇨Printers to open the Printers window.

2. Double-click the printer you're using to open the print queue.

3. Right-click the document you want to stop printing, and then click Cancel from the pop-up menu.

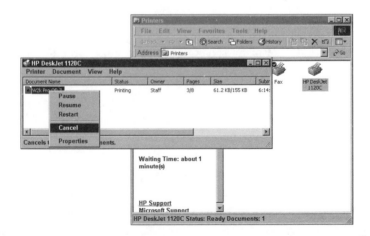

You can cancel the printing of more than one document by holding down the Ctrl key and selecting each document you want to cancel.

Changing the Order of Documents Waiting to Print

Here's how to change the printing order (priority) of documents waiting to print:

1. Choose Start⟳Settings⟳Printers to open the Printers window.

2. Double-click the printer you're using to open the print queue.

3. Right-click the document you want to move in the print order, and then click Properties.

4. On the General tab, drag the Priority slider to raise or lower the document's priority.

 After a document has started printing, you can't change the printing priority of that document.

 To change the printing priority of documents waiting to print, you must have the Manage Documents permission.

Pausing the Printing of a Document

Follow these steps to pause or resume the printing of a document:

1. Choose Start⇨Settings⇨Printers to open the Printers window.

2. Double-click the printer you're using to open the print queue.

3. Right-click the document that you want to pause or resume the printing of.

4. To pause printing, click Pause on the pop-up menu. The document won't print until you resume printing.

5. To resume printing, click Resume on the pop-up menu. The document begins printing. However, if higher-priority documents are waiting to print, they print first.

After a document has started printing, it generally finishes printing, even if you pause it.

Printing a Document

To print a document, follow these steps:

1. Open the document you want to print.

2. Choose File⇨Print. Some applications also have a Print toolbar button.

While the document prints, a printer icon appears next to the clock in the Windows taskbar. When this icon disappears, your document has finished printing.

You can print a document without opening it by dragging its icon to a printer in the Printers folder or to a shortcut on your desktop.

Printing More Than One Copy

Here's how to set the number of copies to print:

1. Choose Start⇨Settings⇨Printers to open the Printers window.

2. Right-click the printer you're using, and then click Printing Preferences.

3. Click Advanced, and under Paper/Output, specify the Copy Count.

 Any changes you make in Printing Preferences affects the default document settings for the printer and all documents you send to the printer.

Printing Multiple Pages on a Sheet

To print multiple pages per sheet, follow these steps:

1. Choose Start⇨Settings⇨Printers to open the Printers window.

2. Right-click the printer you're using and then click Printing Preferences.

3. On the Layout tab, select the number of pages you want to print on a sheet in Pages Per Sheet.

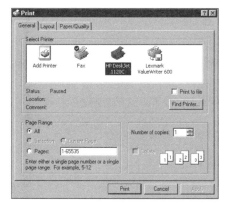

 The Pages Per Sheet option appears in the dialog box only if your printer supports this feature.

Printing on Both Sides of the Paper

Here's how to print on one or both sides of the paper:

1. Choose Start⇨Settings⇨Printers to open the Printers window.

2. Right-click the printer you're using, and then click Printing Preferences.

3. On the Layout tab, under Print on Both Sides (Duplex), click one of the following options:

- **None** to print on only one side of the paper

- **Flip on Short Edge** to print on both sides of the paper with pages that are bound on the top edge

- **Flip on Long Edge** to print on both sides of the paper with pages that are bound on the left edge

The Print on Both Sides (Duplex) options appear in the dialog box only if your printer supports this feature. The specific options available depend on the printer you use.

Restarting the Printing of a Document

To restart printing of a document, follow these steps:

1. Choose Start⇨Settings⇨Printers to open the Printers window.

2. Double-click the printer you're using to open the print queue.

3. Right-click the document that you want to restart printing, and then click Restart from the pop-up menu.

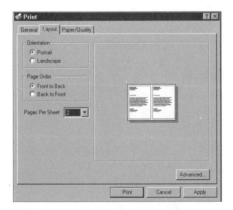

When you restart a document, it starts printing again from the beginning. However, if higher priority documents are in the print queue, they print first.

Selecting Paper Size

Here's how to specify paper size:

1. Choose Start⭢Settings⭢Printers to open the Printers window.

2. Right-click the printer you're using, and then click Printing Preferences.

3. Click Advanced, and under Paper/Output, click Paper Size.

4. Click the paper size you want.

Setting Page Orientation

To set page orientation, follow these steps:

1. Choose Start⭢Settings⭢Printers to open the Printers window.

2. Right-click the printer you're using, and then click Printing Preferences.

3. On the Layout tab, under Orientation, click one of the following options:

- **Portrait** to print vertically on the page

- **Landscape** to print horizontally on the page

- **Rotated Landscape** to rotate the print 90 degrees counter-clockwise on the page

 The Orientation options appear in the dialog box only if your printer supports this feature. The specific options available depend on the printer you use.

Setting Printer Resolution

Follow these steps to set printing resolution:

1. Choose Start⇨Settings⇨Printers to open the Printers window.

2. Right-click the printer you're using, and then click Printing Preferences.

3. Click Advanced, and under Graphic, click Print Quality.

4. Click the resolution option you want.

High-resolution settings produce more dots per inch (dpi) and higher-quality printing, but the settings take longer to print.

Using a Separator Page

If you share a departmental printer, using a separator sheet with your print jobs is a good idea. This makes dividing up a stack of print jobs easier.

Here's how to choose a separator page:

1. Choose Start⇨Settings⇨Printers to open the Printers window.

2. Right-click the printer you're using, and then click Properties.

3. On the Advanced tab, click Separator Page.

4. Click Browse and find your System32 folder.

5. Specify one of the separator page files that Windows 2000 provides in the System32 folder:

- **Pcl.sep**, which prints a page after switching the printer to PCL printing

- **Sysprint.sep**, which prints a page after switching the printer to PostScript printing

- **Pscript.sep**, which does not print a page after switching the printer to PostScript printing

To set up separator pages, you must have the Manage Printers permission.

Viewing Documents Waiting to Print

To view documents waiting to print, follow these steps:

1. Choose Start⇨Settings⇨Printers to open the Printers window.

2. Double-click the printer for which you want to view the documents waiting to print.

The print queue shows information about a document, such as print status, owner, and number of pages to be printed. From the print queue, you can cancel or pause printing for any documents you have sent to the printer.

You can open the print queue for the printer on which you're printing by double-clicking the printer icon on the taskbar.

Part VIII

Networking Near and Far

Windows 2000 Professional extends your reach far and wide with its built-in networking. Whether you want to connect to a computer in the next office, across the campus, or on the other side of the world, Windows 2000 Professional can make the connection. Network and Dial-up Connections connects your computer to the Internet, to a specific network, or to another computer.

In this part . . .

- ✔ Finding out what's on your network
- ✔ Connecting directly to another computer
- ✔ Connecting to computers and printers in your network
- ✔ Connecting to the Internet
- ✔ Sharing your files, folders, and printers on the network
- ✔ Turning off resource sharing

Browsing Your Network

When you start your computer, Windows 2000 finds and identifies your network adapter, and then automatically starts the network connection. The My Network Places folder is what you use to locate shared resources on your computer's network, such as printers, disks, folders, and files.

Because you are connected to the network and the items exist (and are shared), you can access them. Remember, however, that network users depend on network managers to make resources available; if a connection breaks in the server closet, nobody gets anything.

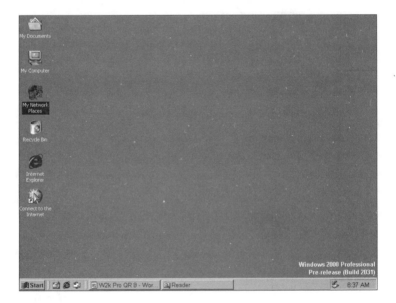

1. Double-click My Network Places on your desktop.

The My Network Places folder opens.

2. Double-click the Entire Network icon in the My Network Places folder.

The Entire Network folder opens.

TIP

If your computer is a member of a workgroup, you can double-click Computers Near Me to narrow your search to computers that are in the same workgroup.

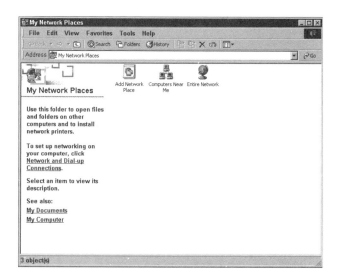

3. To connect to any of the items appearing on your network, see the appropriate section in this part.

Connecting to Another Computer

Sometimes you need a quick and easy connection to a computer that's not a part of your normal network. For example, you might need to connect to a palmtop computer or other computing device that has no network card. In such cases, you can connect to the network directly, using either a cable (serial or parallel) or an infrared link.

To make a direct network connection:

1. Click Start⤳Settings⤳Network and Dial-up Connections.

The Network and Dial-up Connections folder appears.

2. Double-click Make New Connection.

The Network Connection user interface box appears.

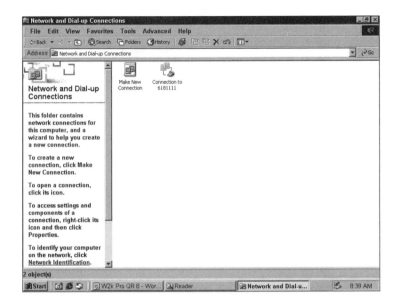

3. Click Next.

The Network Connection Type user interface box appears.

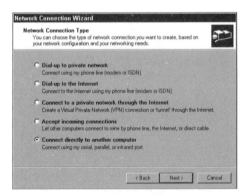

4. Click Connect Directly to Another Computer in the Network Connection Type dialog box, and then click Next.

The Host or Guest user interface box appears.

If you want to serve up data or resources (such as shared printers) from your computer then you're a *host*. If you want to mooch off someone else's computer then you're a *guest*.

To be a host:

1. If you want your computer to receive dial-up connections and act as the host, Select Host and then click Next. This means that your computer contains the information you need to access.

2. Choose a Direct Parallel (LPT1), Communications Port (Com 2), or Infrared Port to connect through from the Device for This Connection list box.

3. Click Next.

The Allowed Users user interface box appears.

4. Select the user(s) you want to allow to connect to your computer. Then click next.

The Network Connection Wizard appears.

5. Enter a name for the connection and click Finish to create and save the connection in the Network and Dial-up Connections folder.

To be a Guest:

1. If you want your computer to dial out, select Guest and then click Next.

This means that another computer has the information you want to access.

2. Choose a Direct Parallel (LPT1), Communications Port (Com 2), or Infrared Port to connect through from the Select a Device list box.

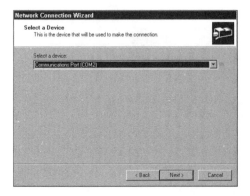

3. Click Next.

The Connection Availability user interface box appears.

4. Select the user(s) you want to allow to connect to your computer, either for all profiles (For all users) or just the current profile (Only for myself), and then click next.

The Network Connection Wizard appears.

5. Enter a name for the connection and click Finish to create and save the connection in the folder for Network and Dial-up Connections.

After you add an infrared device, you may have to restart the computer before you can actually select and use the Infrared Port.

To create a direct network connection, which acts as a host, you must have administrator-level rights.

Connecting to Printers on Your Network

Printers are one of the many resources you might find on your network. Suppose you need a large-format color laser printer to print out your latest presentation and you know there's one on your network. Just locate it and connect to it.

To connect to a printer on a network:

1. Click Start⇨Settings⇨Printers to open Printers.

2. Double-click Add Printer to start the Add Printer wizard, and then click Next.

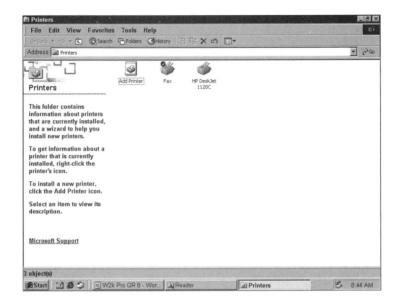

3. Click Network Printer, and then click Next.

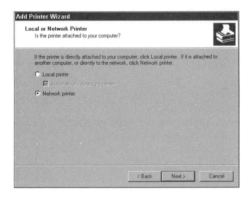

4. Connect to the desired printer using one of the following methods:

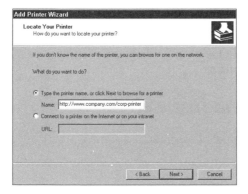

- Type its name in the Name field, using the following format: *printserver_name**share_name*.

  OR

- Type its URL in the URL field, for example: *www.company. com/corp-printer*.

  OR

- Click Next to have the wizard attempt to locate the printer on the network.

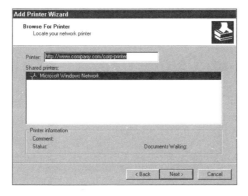

5. Follow the instructions on the screen to finish connecting to the network printer.

The icon for the printer appears in your Printers folder.

If your system administrator allows you to access the print server's Printers folder, you can also connect to a printer by dragging the printer's icon from the print server's Printers folder and dropping it into *your* Printers folder, or by simply right-clicking the icon and then clicking Connect.

Connecting to the Internet

To make an Internet connection:

1. Click Start⇨Settings⇨Network and Dial-up Connections to open Network and Dial-up Connections.

2. Double-click Make New Connection, and then click Next.

3. Click Dial-up to the Internet, click Next, and then follow the instructions in the Network Connection wizard.

 Before you create an Internet connection, check with your Internet service provider (ISP) to verify the required connection settings. A connection to your ISP may require one or more of the following settings:

✦ A specific IP address

✦ IP header compression (for PPP)

✦ DNS addresses and domain names

✦ Optional settings, such as Internet Protocol security

Creating a Dial-up Connection

To set up a connection for the first time:

1. Double-click the My Network Places icon on your desktop. The My Network Places folder appears.

2. Click Start⇨Settings⇨Network and Dial-up Connections. The Network and Dial-up connections folder appears.

3. Double-click the Make a New Connection icon. The Network Connection Wizard appears.

4. Right-click the connection you want to configure, and then click Properties.

5. Do one or more of the following:

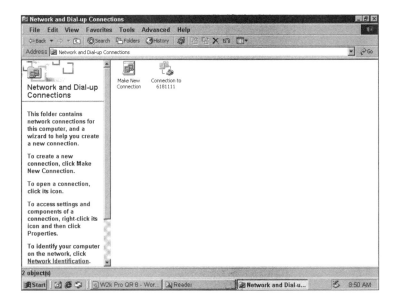

- To configure dialing devices, phone numbers, host address, country codes, or dialing rules, click the General tab.

- To configure dialing and redialing options, multilink configuration, or X.25 parameters, click the Options tab.

- To configure identity authentication, data encryption, or terminal window and scripting options, click the Security tab.

- To configure the dial-up server and protocols used for this connection, click the Networking tab.

- To enable or disable shared access and on-demand dialing, click the Shared Access tab.

Depending on the type of connection you are configuring, different options appear. For example, a local area connection displays only the General tab.

Disconnecting from the Network

To disconnect from the network:

1. Click Start⇨Settings⇨Network and Dial-up Connections to open Network and Dial-up Connections.

2. Right-click the connection you want to disconnect, and then click Disconnect.

Finding Printers on the Network

You know there's a printer out there, but you don't know its name or URL? Let Windows 2000 hunt it down for you!

To use advanced options to search for a printer:

1. Click Start⇨Search⇨For Printers to open Find Printers.

   Be sure that Entire Directory is not selected in the In box.

2. On the Printers and Features tabs, enter the appropriate search information.

3. On the Advanced tab, click Field, and then click the feature or attribute you want to search for (such as Printer Language).

4. In Condition, click the operator you want to use to further define your search — for example, Is (exactly).

5. In Value, type the variable you want to use — for example, Color PostScript — and then click Add.

6. Repeat Steps 4 through 6 until you have entered all your search parameters, and then click Find Now.

The search parameters you defined would find all the printers that support the PostScript printer language.

If you added the Supports Collation field and checked the Is TRUE condition, the search would find all PostScript printers that support collation.

To connect to a printer displayed in the results list, right-click the printer's name and then click Connect (or double-click the name of the printer you want to use).

Serving Incoming Connections

Perhaps you bring work home from the office and find that you need to dial in to your office computer (or vice versa). You can set up either computer to receive calls, allowing you to access either computer — and (if you have the correct permissions) its network resources.

To make an incoming network connection:

1. Click Start⇨Settings⇨Network and Dial-up Connections.

The Network and Dial-up Connections folder appears.

2. Double-click Make New Connection.

The Network Connection user interface box appears.

3. Click Next.

The Network Connection Type user interface box appears.

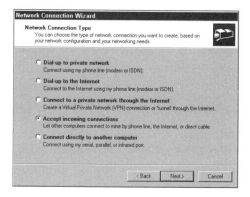

4. Click Accept Incoming Connections, and then click Next.

The Devices for Incoming Connections user interface box appears.

5. Select a modem from the Connection Devices list box and then click Next.

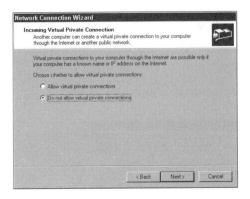

If you do not want another computer to create a virtual private connection to your computer through the Internet or another public network, select Do Not Allow Virtual Private Connections, and then click Next. The Allowed Users user interface box appears.

6. Select the user(s) you want to allow to connect to your computer from the Eligible Users list box and then click Next.

The Networking Components user interface box appears.

7. Select the networking component(s) you want to enable for the connection from the Networking Components list box, choosing from these alternatives:

- Choose Internet Protocol TCP/IP if you plan to connect to the Internet (or other computer network that uses TPC/IP protocol).

- Choose File and Printer Sharing for Microsoft Networks if you want others to be able to access files and printers on your computer.

- This component is installed by default. Client for Microsoft Networks allows you to access shared resources (such as files and printers) on a Microsoft Network.

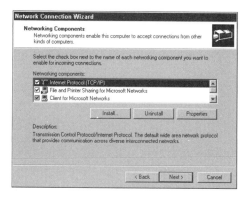

8. Click Next. The Network Connection Wizard appears.

9. Enter a name for the connection, and then click Finish to create and save the connection in the Network and Dial-up Connections folder.

To create an incoming network connection, you must have administrator-level rights.

Setting sharing permissions for drives and folders

Sharing your drive or folders doesn't mean you have to lose control over them. You can decide who will have access to them (and how much) by setting appropriate permissions.

To set, view, or remove permissions for a shared folder or drive:

1. Click Start⇨Programs⇨Accessories⇨Windows Explorer.

2. Locate the shared folder or drive on which you want to set permissions.

3. Right-click the shared folder or drive, and then click Sharing.

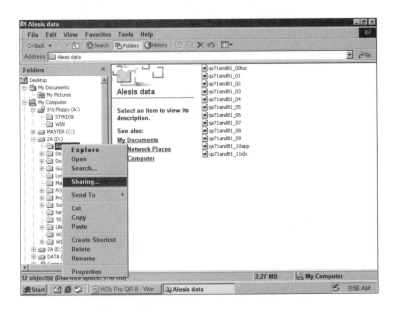

4. On the Sharing tab, click Permissions.

5. Click Add.

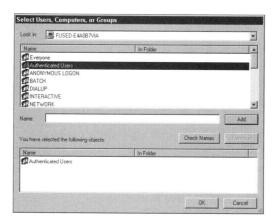

6. In Name, type the name of the group or user you want to set permissions for, click Add, and then click OK to close the dialog box.

7. To remove permissions, select the group or user in Name, and then click Remove.

8. In Permissions, click Allow or Deny for each permission, if necessary.

To share folders and drives, you must be logged on as a member of the Administrators, Server Operators, or Power Users group.

Although they apply to all files and subfolders in the shared folder, shared folder permissions are effective only when the folders or files are reached over a network. Shared permissions do not protect folders or files opened locally.

Setting up File and Printer Sharing

Network services provide features such as file and printer sharing. For example, the File and Printer Sharing for Microsoft Networks service allows other computers to access resources on your computer using a Microsoft network. The following procedure describes how to add a network service to your computer.

1. Click Start⇨Settings⇨Control Panel, and then double-click Network and Dial-up Connections to open Network and Dial-up Connections.

2. Click Local Area Connection, click the File menu, and then click Properties.

3. In the Local Area Connection Properties dialog box, click Install.

4. In the Select Network Component Type dialog box, click Service and then click Add.

5. In the Select Network Service dialog box, click the service you want to install, and then click OK.

Setting up printer-sharing permissions

Keep your printer under control by setting permissions to restrict who uses it and when. If your environment requires that sensitive or confidential material be monitored when printed, set printer-sharing permissions. It's also a way to make sure your printer is available when you have to print out a stack of reports for a crucial meeting.

To set or remove permissions for a printer:

1. Click Start⇨Settings⇨Printers to open Printers.

2. Right-click the name of the printer for which you want to set permissions, click Properties, and then click the Security tab.

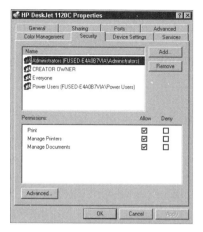

3. Do one of the following:

- To change or remove permissions from an existing user or group, click the name of the user or group.

- To set up permissions for a new user or group, click Add.

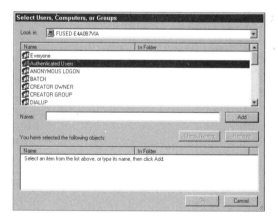

4. In Name, type the name of the user or group you want to set permissions for, click Add, and then click OK to close the dialog box.

5. In Permissions, click Allow or Deny for each type of permission you want to allow or deny, if necessary.

6. To remove the user or group from the permissions list, select the name and click Remove.

WEIRDNESS

To change device settings, you must have the Manage Printers permission.

Sharing your files or folders on the network

The idea of networking is based on sharing tasks as well as resources. You may need to share your work with other members of your workgroup or other departments.

To share a folder or drive with other people:

1. Click Start⇨Programs⇨Accessories, and then click Windows Explorer to open Windows Explorer.

2. Locate the folder or drive you want to share.

3. Right-click the folder or drive you've chosen, and then click Sharing. The Properties dialog box appears.

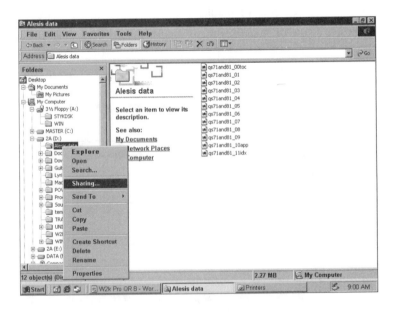

4. On the Sharing tab, click Share This Folder.

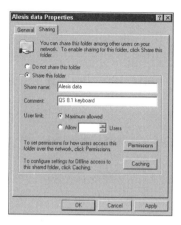

5. To change the name of the shared folder or drive, type a new name in Share name.

Users see the share name when they connect to the shared folder or drive (its actual name does not change).

6. To add a comment about the shared folder or drive, type the text in the space labeled Comment.

7. To limit the number of users who can connect simultaneously to the shared folder or drive, click User limit, click Allow, and then enter a number of users.

8. To set shared folder permissions on the shared folder or drive, click Permissions.

9. To set up this shared folder to be used offline, click Caching.

To share folders and drives, you must be logged on as a member of the Administrators, Server Operators, or Power Users group.

Sharing your printer on the network

To share your printer:

1. Click Start⇨Settings⇨Printers to open Printers.

2. Right-click the name of the printer you want to share, and then click Sharing.

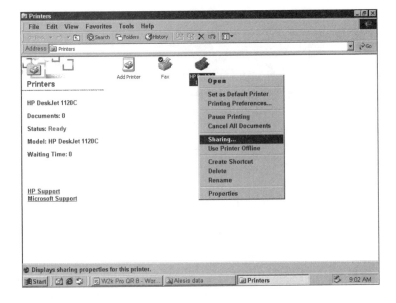

3. On the Sharing tab, click Shared as, and then type a name for the shared printer.

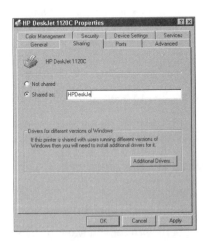

4. If you share the printer with users on different hardware or different operating systems, click Additional Drivers. Click the environment(s) and operating system(s) of the other computers, and then click OK to install the additional drivers.

5. Click OK (or, if you have installed additional drivers, click Close).

Turning off folder sharing

If you decide that you no longer need to allow other users to access your drive or folders, you can turn off sharing.

To stop sharing a folder or drive:

1. Click Start⟹Programs⟹Accessories⟹Windows Explorer to open Windows Explorer.

2. Locate the shared folder or drive you want to stop sharing.

3. Right-click the shared folder or drive, and then click Sharing.

4. On the Sharing tab, click Do Not Share This Folder.

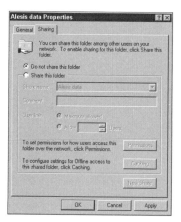

Turning off printer sharing

To stop sharing your printer:

1. Click Start⇨Settings⇨Printers to open Printers.

2. Right-click the printer you want to stop sharing, and then click Sharing.

3. On the Sharing tab, click Not Shared.

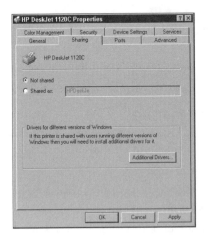

Part IX

Personalizing Your Computer

Windows 2000 provides many ways for you to put the "personal" into "personal computing." It gives you a broad range of choices for customizing your computer environment to suit your work habits and personal preferences. For example, you can change the way things look on the screen and the way programs work, and you can change the behavior of the mouse and keyboard.

In this part . . .

✓ Changing the appearance of items

✓ Adjusting the display

✓ Working with sound and multimedia

✓ Making the computer more accessible

Adding Toolbar Buttons in Folder Windows

1. Choose Start⇨Programs⇨Accessories⇨Windows Explorer to open Windows Explorer.

2. Choose View⇨Toolbars and then click Customize.

- To add a button, select a button from the list of available toolbar buttons and then click Add.

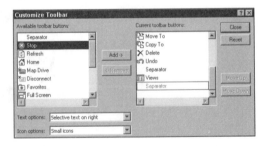

- To remove a button, select a button from the list of current toolbar buttons and then click Remove.

- To restore the toolbar buttons to their default settings, click Reset. This action does not restore the Text Options or the Icon Options to their original settings.

You can also customize the toolbars by right-clicking in the toolbar area and then clicking one or more of the following options:

✦ Standard Buttons

✦ Address Bar

✦ Links

✦ Radio (You must have Windows Media Player installed and you need an Internet connection)

✦ Customize

Adjusting Keyboard Response

FilterKeys adjusts the response of your keyboard.

To turn on FilterKeys:

1. Choose Start⇨Settings⇨Control Panel to open the Control Panel.

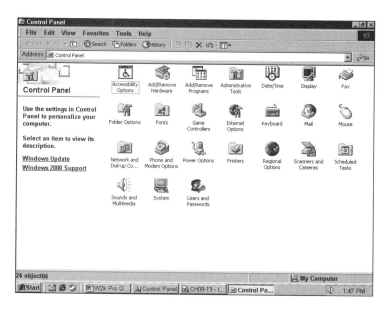

2. Double-click the Accessibility Options icon to open the Accessibility Options dialog box.

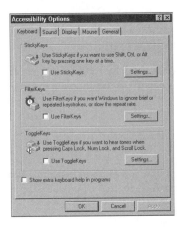

3. On the Keyboard tab, under FilterKeys, select the Use FilterKeys check box.

4. You can change the settings for FilterKeys by choosing Settings.

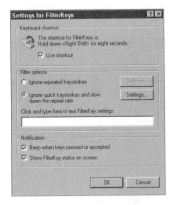

 If you select the Use Shortcut check box in the Settings for FilterKeys dialog box, you can turn FilterKeys on and off by holding down the right Shift key for 8 to 16 seconds. The amount of time depends on the other settings you have selected in the Accessibility Options dialog box.

Adjusting Keystroke Response

The StickyKeys feature enables you to use one key at a time to activate shortcuts that normally require simultaneous keystrokes.

To turn on StickyKeys:

1. Choose Start⇨Settings⇨Control Panel to open the Control Panel.

2. Double-click the Accessibility Options icon to open the Accessibility Options dialog box.

3. On the Keyboard tab, under StickyKeys, select the Use StickyKeys check box.

 You can change the settings for keyboard shortcut, modifier and on/off settings, and notification on the Keyboard menu in the StickyKeys section by choosing Settings.

Adjusting Screen Contrast

High Contrast improves screen contrast with alternative colors and font sizes; this feature helps compensate for visual impairment.

To turn on High Contrast:

1. Choose Start⇨Settings⇨Control Panel to open the Control Panel.

2. Double-click the Accessibility Options icon to open the Accessibility Options dialog box.

3. On the Display tab, under High Contrast, select the Use High Contrast check box.

4. To change settings for High Contrast, choose Settings.

 If you select the Use Shortcut check box in the Settings for the High Contrast dialog box, you can switch the high-contrast scheme on and off by pressing the left Alt+left Shift+Print Screen keys.

Assigning Sounds to Program Events

You can assign various sounds to program events such as program closing, program errors, and so on.

1. Choose Start⇨Settings⇨Control Panel to open the Control Panel.

2. Double-click the and Multimedia icon to open the Sounds and Multimedia Properties dialog box .

3. On the Sounds tab, under Sound Events, click the event to which you want to assign a sound.

4. In the Name drop-down list, click the sound you want to play whenever the selected event occurs.

5. If the sound you want to use is not listed, click Browse.

 You can save your sound settings by clicking Save As and then naming the sound scheme you created. The name you enter will appear in the Scheme list, so you can easily use these settings later.

Changing the System Sound Volume

You can control the loudness of your computer's speaker system through the Sounds and Multimedia applet in the Control Panel.

1. Choose Start⇨Settings⇨Control Panel to open the Control Panel.

2. Double-click the Sounds and Multimedia icon to open the Sounds and Multimedia Properties dialog box.

3. On the Sounds tab, under Sound Volume, drag the slider left or right to decrease or increase the system volume.

 If you select the Show Volume control on the taskbar check box (and your sound card's volume can be changed using software), a speaker icon appears on the taskbar. You can change the volume by clicking that icon and adjusting the slider.

 The volume slider on the Sounds tab is linked to the volume slider in Volume Control. Changing the system volume on the Sounds tab also changes it in Volume Control, and vice versa.

Changing Screen Resolution

A higher screen resolution reduces the size of items on your screen and increases the size of your desktop.

1. Choose Start↷Settings↷Control Panel to open the Control Panel.

2. Double-click the Display icon to open the Display Properties dialog box.

3. On the Settings tab, under Screen area, drag the slider to the desired screen resolution and then click Apply.

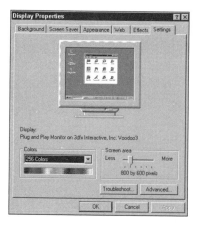

 Your monitor and display adapter determine whether you can change your screen resolution.

Changing the Appearance of Folder Items

1. To open Windows Explorer, click Start, point to Programs, point to Accessories, and then click Windows Explorer.

2. Click the View menu, and then click Large Icons, Small Icons, List, Details, or Thumbnails.

When you use the Details view, you can also select the columns that you want to be visible by choosing View⇨Choose Columns and following the instructions on your screen.

Changing the Look of Desktop Items

1. Choose Start⇨Settings⇨Control Panel to open the Control Panel.

2. Double-click the Display icon to open the Display Properties dialog box.

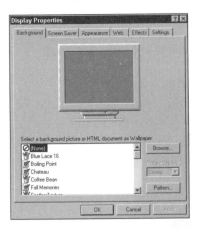

3. In the Item list on the Appearance tab, click the element you want to change, such as Window, Menu, or Scrollbar, and then adjust the appropriate settings, such as color, font, or font size.

• To select a predefined color and font scheme, click an option in the Scheme list.

• To create a customized scheme, select your desired settings in the Item list, click Save As, and then type a name for the scheme. The new scheme will be added to the Scheme list.

Creating a Sound Scheme

The new scheme will appear in the Scheme list so that you can easily use these settings later.

1. Choose Start⇨Settings⇨Control Panel to open the Control Panel.

2. Double-click the Sounds and Multimedia icon to open the Sounds and Multimedia Properties dialog box.

3. On the Sounds tab, under Sound Events, assign a sound for each event you want in a sound scheme.

4. Click Save As and type a name for the new sound scheme.

Customizing a Desktop Pattern

1. Choose Start⇨Settings⇨Control Panel to open the Control Panel.

2. Double-click the Display icon to open the Display Properties dialog box.

3. On the Background tab, click Pattern to open the Pattern dialog box.

4. In the Pattern list, click the desktop pattern you want to modify, and then click Edit Pattern.

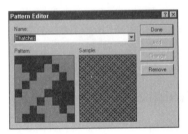

5. Under Name, type a new name for your pattern. Otherwise, the selected pattern will be changed.

6. Under Pattern, click the blocks to reverse the color and change the pattern. Under Sample, you can see the pattern change with each click.

7. Click Add to add your new pattern to the Pattern list, and then click Done.

Displaying Captions

ShowSounds tells programs to display captions for program speech and sounds.

To turn on ShowSounds:

1. Choose Start⇨Settings⇨Control Panel to open the Control Panel.

2. Double-click the Accessibility Options icon to open the Accessibility Options dialog box.

3. On the Sound tab, under ShowSounds, select the Use ShowSounds check box.

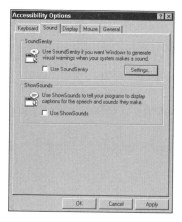

Getting Visual System Warnings

SoundSentry can provide visual warnings for system sounds.

To turn on SoundSentry:

1. Choose Start⇨Settings⇨Control Panel to open the Control Panel.

2. Double-click the Accessibility Options icon to open the Accessibility Options dialog box.

3. On the Sound tab, under SoundSentry, select the Use SoundSentry check box.

4. To change settings for SoundSentry, choose Settings.

Making Folders Look Like Web Pages

When you use Web view, descriptive and hyperlink text appears on the left side of the folder window.

1. Choose Start⇨Settings⇨Control Panel to open the Control Panel.

2. On the General tab, under Web View, click Enable Web content in folders.

To turn off Web view in folders, click Use Windows Classic Folders.

Making the Keyboard Act Like a Mouse

To turn on MouseKeys:

1. Choose Start⇨Settings⇨Control Panel to open the Control Panel.

2. Double-click the Accessibility Options icon to open the Accessibility Options dialog box.

3. On the Mouse tab, under MouseKeys, select the Use MouseKeys check box.

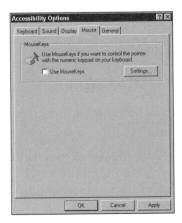

4. To change settings for MouseKeys, choose Settings.

If the Use Shortcut check box in the Settings for MouseKeys dialog box is selected, you can turn MouseKeys on and off by pressing left Alt+left Shift+Num Lock.

Opening Folders in Their Own Windows

By default, each folder you open appears in the same window, replacing the contents of the previous window. You can set folder options so that a new window is opened every time you open a folder.

1. Choose Start⇨Settings⇨Control Panel to open the Control Panel.

2. Double-click the Folder Options icon to open the Folder Options dialog box.

3. On the General tab, under Browse Folders, click Open each folder in its own window.

Setting a Desktop Background

1. Choose Start⇨Settings⇨Control Panel to open the Control Panel.

2. Double-click the Display icon to open the Display Properties dialog box.

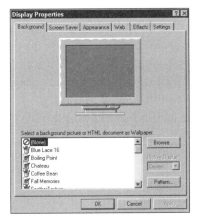

3. On the Background tab, do one or more of the following:

   • In the Picture Display list, click Center, Tile, or Stretch.

   • Select a background picture from the wallpaper list.

     Background pictures may have the following file extensions: .bmp, .gif, .jpg, .dib, or .htm.

Setting a Screen Saver

1. Choose Start⇨Settings⇨Control Panel to open the Control Panel.

2. Double-click the Display icon to open the Display Properties dialog box.

3. On the Screen Saver tab, under Screen Saver, click a screen saver in the list.

   To view possible setting options for a particular screen saver, click Settings on the Screen Saver tab.

- After you select a screen saver, it will automatically start when your computer is idle for the number of minutes specified in Wait.

- To clear the screen saver after it has started, move your mouse or press any key. Or, if you have assigned a screen saver password, type your logon password.

ToggleKeys

ToggleKeys emits sounds to alert you when certain locking keys are pressed.

To turn on ToggleKeys:

1. Choose Start➪Settings➪Control Panel to open the Control Panel.

2. Double-click the Accessibility Options icon to open the Accessibility Options dialog box.

3. On the Keyboard tab, under ToggleKeys, select the Use ToggleKeys check box.

4. You can change settings for ToggleKeys by selecting the Settings button.

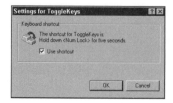

If the Use Shortcut check box in the Settings for ToggleKeys dialog box is selected, you can turn ToggleKeys on and off by holding down the Num Lock key for five seconds.

Using the Active Desktop Feature

1. Choose Start➪Settings➪Control Panel to open the Control Panel.

Or, in Windows Explorer, click Tools and then click Folder Options.

2. On the General tab, under Active Desktop, click Enable Web content on My Desktop.

Techie Talk

authentication: A computer running Windows 2000 Professional goes through this process to make sure that you are who you say you are. After a user logs on to an account on a computer running Windows 2000 Professional, the computer tries to match your username with your password against a list of authorized users. After a user logs on to an account on a Windows 2000 Professional Server domain, any server of that domain may perform the authentication.

backup domain controller: A computer that receives a copy of the Windows 2000 Server domain's security policy and domain database. The computer uses this information to authenticate network logons.

Browse: Just like you do when you're window shopping, this feature allows you to look through lists of directories, files, user accounts, groups, domains, or computers.

channel: A Web site designed to deliver content from the Internet to your computer. Just like TV, you tune in or subscribe to a favorite Web site. With channels, the content provider can suggest a schedule for your subscription, or you can customize your own.

client: A computer that accesses shared-network resources provided by another computer (called a server) — usually at no charge to the client, although you may want to set up a service charge to earn extra money.

Clipboard: A temporary storage space within the computer's memory in which you can save text or graphics for later reuse. You place items on the Clipboard by using the Cut or Copy commands within an application. To use (or even reuse) an item you've placed on the Clipboard, use the Paste command.

computer name: A unique name of up to 15 characters that identifies a computer to the network. The name cannot be the same as any other computer or domain name in the network.

Content Advisor: Internet Explorer's way of screening the types of content that your computer can access on the Internet. After you turn on Content Advisor, only rated content that meets or exceeds your criteria can be displayed.

cursor: The little arrow-shaped bar that follows you around the screen when you move the mouse. (Cursors can have other shapes. Some are shaped like dinosaurs, for example.)

directory: Areas on a disk used to store files. Directories are called folders in Windows 2000 Professional.

document: A document is what an application displays in its window. If you're using a word processor, for example, a document may be a letter, memo, fax, or other work.

domain: For a Windows 2000 Professional server, a domain is a collection of computers that share a common account database and security policy. Each domain has a unique name.

domain controller: Every Windows 2000 Professional Server domain has a server — the domain controller — that authenticates or validates domain logons and maintains the security policy and the master database for a domain.

domain name: The name by which a domain is known to the network.

double-click: To click twice very fast.

drag and drop: A technique that allows you to move or copy files or pieces of documents by using the mouse. Select the item you want to move or copy with your mouse, drag it, and release it where you want it.

Encrypted File System (EFS): Windows 2000 Professional offers more heightened security than Windows 95 and Windows NT Workstation 4.0. If users store sensitive information on a mobile computer, they can encrypt those files and folders. If the laptop is stolen, EFS protects its files and folders, even if the thief reinstalls Windows 2000 Professional. Only users with a special decryption key can access the file.

EFS provides only local encryption. If a file is sent over a network, for example, encryption must be handled differently, such as through IPsec or other network security technologies.

event: A happening in Windows 2000 Professional, such as printing a document or starting a Windows 2000 Professional service.

FAT: Stands for *file allocation table,* which is a table or list maintained by some operating systems to keep track of the status of various segments or portions of disk space used for file storage.

folder: You knew folders as directories under DOS. A folder is an area on a disk where files are stored.

Hal (Hardware Abstraction Layer): Enables Windows 2000 Professional to work with different types of hardware (serves like a mediator between two sides that can't get along).

hardware profile: A set of instructions that tells Windows 2000 which devices to start when you start your computer and what settings to use for each device. The major advantage of a hardware profile is being able to create multiple profiles and choosing one at boot-up. This feature mostly helps mobile users who take their computers home or on the road and have access to different devices like modems, printers, and so on.

hibernate mode: Turns off all power to the computer for an indefinite time while maintaining the state of open programs and connected hardware when the computer went into hibernation. Simply put, when you restart and log back in, everything is where you left it.

icon: Those cute little pictures that litter your desktop. An icon represents programs, folders, or data files.

Local Group: Used for security with Windows 2000 Professional. A Local Group is comprised of users that have permission to use a Windows 2000 Professional directory or printer. The term *Local* refers to the computer to which the user connects.

maximize: To increase a taskbar item or window so that it takes up the full screen.

minimize: To shrink a window to an item on the taskbar.

MS-DOS-based application: An application designed to run with plain ol' MS-DOS. Therefore, the application may not be able to take full advantage of all Windows 2000 Professional features.

network: A collection of computers and peripheral devices connected together via cabling.

non-Windows 2000 Professional application: An application designed to run with those other operating systems like Windows 3.*x*, MS-DOS, OS/2, or POSIX, but not specifically with Windows 2000 Professional. Note that applications designed to run on Windows 95 usually run without a hitch on Windows 2000 Professional and take full advantage of all the Windows 2000 Professional features.

NTFS: An advanced file system designed for use specifically by the Windows NT and Windows 2000 Professional operating systems. It supports file system recovery, extremely large storage media, and a slew of other goodies.

offline browsing: You can view Web pages without being connected to the Internet. This feature is handy if you don't always have access to the Web when you want to browse Web pages. You may be using your laptop computer at a location that does not provide any network or modem access. Or you may be at home and not want to tie up your only phone line.

partition: A logical storage element. A partition can be a portion of a hard disk, an entire hard disk, or multiple hard disks that work together to store data.

password: A unique string of characters that must be provided before a logon or an access is authorized. A password is a security measure used to restrict logons to user accounts and access to computer systems and resources. For Windows 2000 Professional, a password for a user account can be up to 14 characters and is case-sensitive.

permissions: Assigning a user rights to use a Windows 2000 Professional file, directory, or printer. These rights include no-access permissions, read-only permissions, change permissions, and full-access permissions.

print job: A document sent to the printer. A print job is the smallest element that you can move, pause, or delete by using the Print Manager.

Profile Assistant: Internet Explorer's way of letting Web sites know who you are and where you are. Profile Assistant can send registration and demographic information to Web sites that require this information so that you don't have to repeatedly enter the same information, such as your e-mail address or postal address, every time you visit a new Web site. None of this information can be viewed on your computer, or shared with others, without your permission.

protocol: Software that follows specific rules to communicate over a network, such as NetBEUI, TCP/IP, and NWLink.

Registry: A secure file that Windows 2000 Professional uses to write configuration information about itself.

resource: Any part of a computer system or a network, such as a disk drive, printer, or memory, that can be accessed or used.

security certificates: A *certificate* is a statement guaranteeing the identity of a person or the security of a Web site. A *personal certificate* is a kind of guarantee that you are who you say you are. A *Web site certificate* states that a specific Web site is secure and genuine.

server: In general, a computer that provides shared resources to network users. In some specific cases, refers to a computer that runs a Windows 2000 Professional server but is not a primary domain controller or a backup domain controller of a Windows 2000 Professional domain.

service: A process that performs a specific system function and often provides an application programming interface (API) for other processes to call.

share: An element of Windows 2000 Professional that others are allowed to use, such as printers and directories.

striped set: Combining multiple hard-disk partitions to make a large storage area providing high performance. With a striped set, Windows 2000 Professional splits files that you save across multiple hard disks and reads them back in proper sequence. Writing and reading files in this fashion is very fast, because files can be written and read much more quickly when split across multiple hard disks than they can when they are written to and read from a single hard disk.

Suspend mode: Puts the system into a deep sleep, with some power. Waking from Suspend mode takes only a few seconds yet can add hours to a laptop computer's battery life.

Synchronization Manager: The new Synchronization Manager tool in Windows 2000 Professional can synchronize all network resources, including files, folders, e-mail, and databases, in a single location.

Taskbar: The bar that lists all currently running programs and open folders.

Understanding User Profile: Defines customized desktop environments, which include individual display settings, network and printer connections, and other specified settings. You or your system administrator may define your desktop environment.

user account: Consists of all the information that defines a user to Windows 2000 Professional (similar to a dossier). This information includes the username and password required for the user to log on, the groups in which the user account has membership, and the rights and permissions the user has for using the system and accessing its resources.

username: A unique name identifying a user account to Windows 2000 Professional. An account's username cannot be identical to any other group name or username on its own domain or workgroup.

volume: A formatted hard disk partition that either contains files or is ready to contain files. Volumes appear as disk drives in My Computer. Mapped network folders or drives also appear as volumes.

volume set: Combining multiple volumes together to create a large hard-disk storage area. Using the Disk Administrator, you can combine multiple partitions that enable you to store more information than a single hard disk can hold.

workgroup: A moderately-sized conglomeration of computers on a local network set up to share similar resources and access. A unique name identifies each workgroup.

workstation: Computers running the Windows 2000 Professional operating system are called workstations, to distinguish them from computers running Windows 2000 Server or Advanced Server, which can be domain servers and controllers.

Index

Numbers

3D Pinball, described, 56, 63

A

Accessibility Options dialog box, 145–146
Active Desktop feature, 156
Add Printer Wizard, 106–107, 126–128
Add/Remove Programs applet
  adding/removing Windows 2000 accessories, 57
  program installation process, 48–49
  removing programs from your system, 51
address book
  accessing from Outlook Express, 98
  adding e-mail contacts to, 93–94
  vCard creation, 95–96
Administrators Group, add a printer, 107
Alt key
  command selection techniques, 18
  dialog box item selection techniques, 8
  switching between open applications, 54
applications. *See also* programs
  launching by opening a file, 36
  switching between, 54
associations, file type, 24
attachments
  e-mail, 98
  saving, 100
  sending pictures with e-mail, 100–101

audio CDs, CD Player playback process, 60–61
authentication, described, 157
automatically adding printer, 106

B

Back button, Help system navigation, 10
backgrounds
  colors, Internet Explorer settings, 80–81
  desktop, 69, 155
backup domain controller, described, 157
backups, described, 27
bookmarking, described, 78–79
browse, described, 157
Browse for Folder dialog box, described, 29, 35
bullets, described, 75
business cards, vCard format creation, 95–96
buttons
  adding in folder window, 144–145
  described, 7
  removing, 144

C

Calculator
  described, 57–60
  math functions, 58
  number system conversions, 60
  scientific functions, 59–60
  statistical functions, 59
Call⇨Connect command, 64
captions, displaying, 152–153
Capture Text dialog box, described, 65–66

CD Player, described, 56, 60–61
certificate, described, 161
channel, described, 158
Character Map, described, 57, 61–62
check boxes, dialog box element,
    8–9
clicking, described, 13
client, described, 158
Clipboard, described, 158
Close button (X), described, 8
color schemes, creating custom, 150
colors, Web page background, 80–81
commands
  Call⇨Connect, 64
  Control-menu, 17
  Edit⇨Copy, 28
  Edit⇨Copy to Folder, 28, 95
  Edit⇨Cut, 34
  Edit⇨Find, 74
  Edit⇨Move to Folder, 35, 97
  Edit⇨Paste, 28, 34
  Edit⇨Undo, 74
  File⇨Create Shortcut, 46
  File⇨Delete, 31
  File⇨Empty Recycle Bin, 31
  File⇨Exit, 50
  File⇨Export⇨Business Card
    (vCard), 95
  File⇨Folder⇨Delete, 97
  File⇨Folder⇨New, 94
  File⇨New Connection, 63
  File⇨New Folder, 30
  File⇨Open, 36, 64
  File⇨Page Setup, 69
  File⇨Print, 69, 112
  File⇨Print Preview, 69, 76
  File⇨Properties, 40
  File⇨Rename, 25
  File⇨Save Attachments, 100
  File⇨Save Search, 33
  File⇨Send To⇨3½ Floppy (A), 26
  File⇨Set as Wallpaper
    (Centered), 69
  File⇨Set as Wallpaper (Tiled), 69
  Format⇨Apply Stationery, 103
  Format⇨Bullet Style, 75

  Format⇨Font, 75
  Format⇨Rich Text (HTML), 101
  Insert⇨Date and Time, 74
  Insert⇨File Attachment, 100
  Insert⇨Picture, 100
  Message⇨Forward, 97
  Message⇨New Message Using, 103
  Programs⇨Accessories, 56
  selecting from a menu, 18
  Send To, 38–39
  Send To⇨3½ Floppy (A), 27
  Settings⇨Control Panel, 48
  shortcut menu selection
    techniques, 19
  Start⇨Programs, 53
  Start⇨Programs⇨Accessories⇨
    Windows Explorer, 144
  Start⇨Run, 52
  Start⇨Search⇨For Printers, 130
  Start⇨Settings⇨Control Panel, 145
  Start⇨Settings⇨Network and Dial-
    up Connections, 121
  Start⇨Settings⇨Printers,
    106–107, 110, 125
  Tools⇨Add Sender to Address
    Book, 93–94
  Tools⇨Address Book, 98
  Tools⇨Options⇨Compose, 96, 102
  Tools⇨Options⇨Send, 93
  Tools⇨Spelling, 95
  Transfer⇨Capture Text, 65
  Transfer⇨Capture to Printer, 66
  Transfer⇨Receive File, 65
  Transfer⇨Send File, 64
  Transfer⇨Send Text File, 64
  View⇨Arrange Icons, 39
  View⇨Choose Columns, 150
  View⇨Options, 75
  View⇨Scientific, 59
  View⇨Thumbnails, 42
  View⇨Toolbars, 144
computer name, described, 158
computers
  adding printers, 106–110
  Network Connection Wizard,
    122–125

program installation process,
48–49
removing programs from, 51
serving incoming connections,
130–142
shutting down properly, 14–15
Confirm File Delete message box,
described, 31
contacts, adding to your address
book, 93–94
Content Advisor, described, 158
Control Panel
adding/removing accessory
programs, 57
network file/printer share
settings, 136
program installation process,
48–49
removing programs from your
system, 51
Control-menu commands,
described, 17
copies, printing multiple, 112–113
Create Shortcut Wizard, described,
47–48
Ctrl key
file/folder selection techniques, 28
Recycle Bin file/folder selection
techniques, 31
Ctrl+Alt+Delete keys, Windows
2000 Professional startup
requirement, 16
cursor, described, 158
customization
appearance of folder items, 150
caption display, 152–153
desktop items appearance, 150–151
desktop pattern, 151–152
folders open in separate windows,
154–155
keyboard response, 145–146
keyboard to act as mouse, 154
keystroke response, 147
making folders look like Web
pages, 153
screen contrast, 147

screen resolution, 149
screen savers, 155–156
setting desktop background, 155
sound scheme, 151
sounds for program events, 148
system sound volume, 148–149
ToggleKeys, 156
toolbar buttons, 144–145
visual system warnings, 153
Customize Toolbar dialog box,
Internet Explorer settings,
81–82

D

Date and Time dialog box,
described, 74
desktop
active feature, 156
changing appearance of items,
150–151
customizing pattern, 151–152
described, 6–7
screen elements, 6–7
setting background, 155
shortcut creation, 46
using pictures as, 69
Web page as wallpaper, 87
desktop patterns, customizing,
151–152
dialog boxes
button elements, 7
check box selections, 8–9
closing properly, 8
described, 7–9
ellipsis (...) character, 7
Help system techniques, 10–11
item selection techniques, 8–9
list box selections, 9
message information display, 7–8
warning information display, 7
Dial-Up Connections, creating,
128–129
directory, described, 158
disks, selection techniques, 14

Display Properties dialog box, 149–150

displaying, captions, 152–153

doc(Word 2000) file extension, 24

documents
canceling printing, 110–111
changing print order, 111
described, 158
inserting special characters, 61–62
pausing printing, 112
printing, 112–115
restarting printing, 114–115
using separator page, 116
waiting to print, 117
WordPad creation, 73

Documents menu, clearing documents from, 49

domain, described, 158

domain controller, described, 158

domain name, described, 158

double-clicking, described, 13, 158

drag and drop, described, 13, 158

drives
disabling share settings, 141
network permissions, 134–136

drop-down list box, described, 9

DVD drives, audio CD playback, 60–61

E

Edit➪Copy command, 28

Edit➪Copy to Folder command, 28, 95

Edit➪Cut command, 34

Edit➪Find command, 74

Edit➪Move to Folder command, 35, 97

Edit➪Paste command, 28, 34

Edit➪Undo command, 74

effects, sound file altering, 70–71

ellipsis (...) character, dialog box element, 7

e-mail
adding contacts to your address book, 93–94
attachments, 98
copying messages to another folder, 95
forwarding a message, 97
ISP account information, 90–92
message deletion, 97
message priority assignments, 94–95
moving messages, 97
printing a message, 99
reading messages, 99
replying to a message, 99
saving a file attachment, 100
saving messages, 100
sending a file attachment, 100
sending messages, 101
sending messages on stationery, 101–103
sending pictures as attachments, 100–101
sending Web pages as, 86–87
spell checking messages, 95
vCard creation, 95–96

Encrypted File System (EPS), described, 159

Esc button, closing a dialog box, 8

event, described, 159

F

FAT (file allocation table), described, 159

File➪Create Shortcut command, 46

File➪Delete command, 31

File➪Empty Recycle Bin command, 31

File➪Exit command, 50

File➪Export➪Business Card (vCard) command, 95

File➪Folder➪Delete command, 97

File➪Folder➪New command, 94

File➪New Connection command, 63

File➪New Folder command, 30

File➪Open command, 36, 64

File➪Page Setup command, 69
File➪Print command, 69, 112
File➪Print Preview command, 69, 76
File➪Properties command, 40
File➪Rename command, 25
File➪Save Attachments command, 100
File➪Save Search command, 33
File➪Send To➪3½ Floppy (A)
   command, 26
File➪Set as Wallpaper (Centered)
   command, 69
File➪Set as Wallpaper (Tiled)
   command, 69
file extensions
  DOC (Word 2000), 24
  LOG (Notepad), 67–68
files
  associating by type, 24
  backup copies, 27–29
  copying between drives/folders,
    27–29
  copying to a floppy disk, 26–27
  deleting, 30–31
  deleting without moving to the
    Recycle Bin, 36–37
  e-mail attachments, 98
  graphic thumbnail viewing, 42
  list view, 41–42
  media, 66–67
  MIME-encoded, 86
  moving, 34–35
  naming conventions, 24–25
  network share settings, 136–139
  opening, 36
  receiving from a remote
    computer, 64–65
  renaming, 24–25
  retrieving from the Recycle Bin,
    37–38
  saving Web page as, 85–86
  selection techniques, 14
  sending to a remote computer, 64
  sending to other destinations,
    38–39
  sorting techniques, 39–40
  viewing properties, 40–41

FilterKeys, turning on, 145–146
Find: All Files dialog box, file/folder
  search, 32–33
floppy disks, copying a file to, 26–27
folder items, changing
  appearance, 150
Folder Options dialog box, 154
folder windows, adding toolbar
  buttons, 144–145
folders
  appear like Web pages, 153
  copying, 27–29
  creating, 29–30
  deleting, 30–31, 97
  described, 159
  disabling share settings, 141
  moving, 34–35
  My Documents, 35
  My Network Places, 120–121
  naming conventions, 24–25, 30
  network permissions, 134–136
  network share settings, 138–139
  opening in own window, 154–155
  Outlook Express creation, 94
  renaming, 24–25
  selection techniques, 14
fonts
  Internet Explorer settings, 80–81
  WordPad settings, 75
Format➪Apply Stationery
  command, 103
Format➪Bullet Style command, 75
Format➪Font command, 75
Format➪Rich Text (HTML)
  command, 101
Found New Hardware Wizard, 106
Freecell, described, 57, 62–63

G

games
  3D Pinball, 57, 62–63
  Freecell, 57, 62–63
  Minesweeper, 57, 62–63
  Solitaire, 57, 62–63

graphics
  disabling for faster Web page
    display, 83
  thumbnail viewing, 42
guests, described, 122

H

Hal (Hardware Abstraction Layer),
    described, 159
hardware profile, described, 159
Help system
  accessing, 12
  Contents tab navigation, 12–13
  described, 9–13
  dialog box settings, 10–11
  exiting properly, 10
  navigation techniques, 10
  search techniques, 10–12
  topic printing, 11
hibernate mode, described, 159
home page, Internet Explorer
    settings, 82
hosts, described, 122
HyperTerminal
  connection setup, 63–64
  described, 56
  port settings, 65
  printing sessions, 66
  receiving files from a remote
    computer, 64–65
  remote computer dial-up
    process, 64
  remote computer file transfers, 64
  saving a communications session
    to a file, 65–66
  startup process, 63

1

icon, described, 6, 159
Imaging, described, 56
Insert⇨Date and Time command, 74

Insert⇨File Attachment
    command, 100
Insert⇨Picture command, 100
Internet, network connection
    process, 128–129
Internet Accounts dialog box, mail/
    news account information,
    90–92
Internet Connection Wizard, mail/
    news account information,
    91–92
Internet Explorer
  bookmarking a Web page, 78–79
  copying information from a Web
    page, 83
  described, 6
  disabling graphics for faster
    display, 83
  font settings, 80–81
  home page display settings, 82
  Links Bar, 78
  MIME-encoded file, 86
  offline Web page browsing,
    79–80, 87
  printing a Web page, 84–85
  saving a Web page to a file, 85–86
  search techniques, 83–84
  sending Web pages as e-mail,
    86–87
  shortcut creation, 83
  toolbar settings, 81–82
  using a Web page as desktop
    wallpaper, 87
Internet Options dialog box, home
    page settings, 82
ISP (Internet Service Provider)
  connection information, 128
  mail/news account information,
    90 –92
items
  dialog box selection techniques,
    8–9
  selection techniques, 14
  Start menu display, 15
  Windows Explorer elements, 42–43

J

jumps, Help system navigation, 10

K

keyboards
act like a mouse, 154
adjusting response, 145–146
keystrokes, adjusting response,
146–147

L

landscape orientation, 115
links
described, 78
sending as e-mail, 86–87
Links Bar, adding a Web page to, 78
list boxes, dialog box element, 9
Local Group, described, 159
log (Notepad) file extension, 67–68
log on, Windows 2000 Professional
startup requirement, 16
logs, Notepad uses, 67–68

M

mail accounts, ISP information,
90–92
math functions, Calculator, 58
maximize, described, 159
media files, opening/playing, 66–67
Media Player
described, 57, 66–67
opening/playing a media file, 66–67
starting, 66
menu bar, described, 18
menus
command selection techniques, 18
described, 18–19
Message↪Forward command, 97
Message↪New Message Using
command, 103

messages
copying, 95
deleting, 97
dialog box element, 7–8
forwarding, 97
moving, 97
Outlook Express e-mail priority
assignments, 94–95
posting to a newsgroup, 98
printing, 99
reading, 99
replying to, 99
saving a copy, 100
sending, 101
sending on stationery, 101–103
spell checking prior to sending as
e-mail, 95
MIME-encoded file, described, 86
Minesweeper, described, 57, 62–63
minimize, described, 159
modems, HyperTerminal port
settings, 65
mouse
clicking, 13
command selection techniques, 18
double-clicking, 13
drag and drop file copying
technique, 27–28
dragging, 13
item selection techniques, 14
keyboard as, 154
moving files/folders, 34–35
right-clicking, 13–14
MouseKeys, enabling, 154
MS-DOS-based application,
described, 160
MS-DOS programs
quitting properly, 49
startup process, 52
My Computer
copying a file to a floppy disk,
26–27
described, 6
file sorting, 39–40
file/folder deletion, 30–31
folder creation/naming, 29–30

My Computer *(continued)*
  graphic file thumbnail viewing, 42
  launching an application when
    opening a file, 36
  moving files/folders, 34–35
  renaming files/folders, 24–25
My Documents folder, described, 6, 35
My Network Places
  described, 6
  network browsing, 120–121

N

Network Connection Wizard
  described, 122–125
  serving incoming connections,
    131–134
networks
  Add Printer Wizard, 125–128
  browsing, 120–121
  connecting to another computer,
    121–125
  described, 160
  disabling share settings, 141–142
  disconnecting from, 129
  drive/folder permissions, 134–136
  file/printer share settings, 136–142
  host/guest relationship, 122–125
  Internet connections, 128–129
  Network Connection Wizard,
    122–125, 131–134
  printer connections, 125–128
  printer search, 130
  serving incoming connections,
    130–142
news accounts, ISP account
  information, 90–92
newsgroups
  posting a message to, 98
  replying to a message, 99
non-windows 2000 Professional
  application, described, 160
Notepad
  described, 57, 67–68
  log uses, 67–68
  starting, 67

NTFS, described, 160
number systems, Calculator
  conversions, 60

O

offline browsing, described, 160
Offline Favorite Wizard, described,
  79–80
online help, described, 9–13
Outlook Express
  accessing the address book, 98
  adding contacts to the address
    book, 93–94
  business card creation, 95–96
  copying messages, 95
  deleting messages, 97
  e-mail message reply, 99
  file attachments, 98
  folder creation, 94, 97
  forwarding messages, 97
  ISP mail/news account
    information, 90–92
  message priority assignments,
    94–95
  moving messages, 97
  newsgroup message reply, 99
  posting messages to a
    newsgroup, 98
  printing a message, 99
  reading messages, 99
  saving a file attachment, 100
  saving a message copy, 100
  sending a file attachment, 100
  sending e-mail message, 101
  sending pictures as attachments,
    100–101
  spell checking messages, 95
  stationery, 101–103
  vCard creation, 95–96

P

page orientation, setting, 115
pages, printing both sides, 114

Pages Per Sheet option, 113
Paint
  described, 56, 68–69
  opening an existing file, 68–69
  printing pictures, 69
  starting, 68
  using picture as desktop
    background, 69
paper size, selecting, 115
partition, described, 160
password
  described, 160
  Windows 2000 Professional
    startup requirement, 16
Pattern dialog box, 151
permissions
  described, 160
  file/printer share settings, 136–142
  network drives/folders, 134–136
personal certificate, described, 161
pictures
  printing, 69
  sending as e-mail attachment,
    100–101
  setting as desktop background, 69
portrait orientation, 115
ports, HyperTerminal settings, 65
print job, described, 160
Print On Both Sides (Duplex)
    option, 114
print queue, checking, 117
Print sharing dialog box, 108
Print Test Page dialog box, 108
printer resolution, setting, 116
printers
  Add Printer Wizard, 126–128
  adding to computer, 106–110
  Administrators Group login, 107
  disabling share settings, 142
  network connections, 125–128
  network search, 130
  network share settings, 136–138
  setting resolution, 116
printing
  both sides of paper, 114
  canceling, 110

changing order, 111
documents, 112
e-mail messages, 99
Help topics, 11
HyperTerminal sessions, 66
multiple copies, 112–113
multiple pages on a sheet, 113
page orientation, 115
pausing, 112
pictures, 69
restarting, 114–115
select paper size, 115
separator page use, 116
test pages, 108–109
viewing documents waiting list, 117
Web pages, 84–85
WordPad documents, 75–76
priorities, Outlook Express mes-
    sage importance assignments,
    94–95
Profile Assistant, described, 160–161
program events, assigning
    sounds, 148
programs. *See also* applications
  adding to the Programs menu, 47
  adding to the Start menu, 47–48
  exiting properly, 49–50
  removing from your system, 51
  Run command startup, 52–53
  Start button startup process, 53
  starting from MS-DOS, 52
  starting when accessing Windows
    2000 Professional, 53–54
  switching between open
    applications, 54
  system installation process,
    48–49
Programs⇨Accessories command, 56
Programs menu, adding programs
    to, 47
properties, described, 40–41
Properties dialog box, described,
    40–41
protocol, described, 161
publications, *Everyday Math For
    Dummies*, 57

R

Receive File dialog box, remote computer file transfers, 65
Recycle Bin
  described, 6, 36
  emptying, 31
  permanently deleting files, 36–37
  resizing, 25–26
  retrieving deleted files/shortcuts, 37–38
Recycle Bin Properties dialog box, resizing the Recycle Bin, 25–26
Registry, described, 161
remote computer
  file transfers, 64
  HyperTerminal dial-up, 64
  receiving files from, 64–65
  serving incoming connections, 130–142
resolution
  screen, 149
  setting printer, 116
resource, described, 161
right-clicking, described, 13–14
rotated landscape orientation, 115
Run dialog box, described, 52–53

S

Save Search dialog box, described, 33
Save Web Page dialog box, described, 85–86
scientific functions, Calculator, 59–60
screen contrast, adjusting, 147–148
screen resolution, changing, 149
screen savers, setting, 155–156
scroll bars, described, 19
Search dialog box, Help system topic search, 11–12
Search Results dialog box, described, 33
Search submenu, file/folder search, 32–33
searches
  file/folder, 32–33
  Help system, 10–12
  network printers, 130
  saving search results, 33
  Web page techniques, 83–84
  WordPad, 74
security, startup password, 16
security certificates, described, 161
Send File dialog box, remote computer file transfers, 64
Send To⇨3½ Floppy (A) command, 27
Send To command, 38–39
Send To folder, sending files to other destinations, 38–39
separator page, using, 116
server, described, 161
service, described, 161
Settings⇨Control Panel command, 48
Settings for MouseKeys dialog box, 154
share, described, 161
shortcut icons, described, 7
shortcut menus, described, 19–20
shortcuts
  adding to the desktop, 46
  Ctrl key to cancel printing, 111
  MouseKeys on/off, 154
  removing from the Start menu, 50–51
  retrieving from the Recycle Bin, 37–38
  Web page creation, 83
Show Volume Control, changing volume, 149
ShowSounds feature, 152–153
Shut Down Windows dialog box, described, 14–15
Solitaire, described, 57, 62–63

sound files
  altering, 70–71
  opening/playing in Sound
    Recorder, 70
  recording/saving, 70
Sound Recorder
  altering sound files, 70–71
  described, 57, 69–71
  opening/playing a sound file, 70
  recording/saving sounds, 70
  starting, 69–70
sound schemes, creating, 151
sounds
  assigning to program events, 148
  changing system volume, 148–149
  creating scheme, 151
  saving settings, 148
  Volume Control settings, 71–72
Sounds and Multimedia applet, 148
Sounds and Multimedia Properties
    dialog box, 148
SoundSentry feature, 153
spell checking, Outlook Express
    e-mail messages, 95
Start⇨Programs⇨Accesso-
    ries⇨Windows Explorer
    command, 144
Start⇨Programs command, 53
Start⇨Run command, 52
Start⇨Search⇨For Printers
    command, 130
Start⇨Settings⇨Control Panel
    command, 145
Start⇨Settings⇨Network and Dial-
    up Connections command, 121
Start⇨Settings⇨Printers command,
    106–107, 110, 125
Start button
  described, 6
  program startup process, 53
Start menu
  adding programs to, 47
  item display, 15
  removing programs from, 50–51

Startup folder, automatic program
    startup settings, 53–54
stationery, Outlook Express e-mail
    message enhancements,
    101–103
statistical functions, Calculator, 59
StickyKeys feature, 146–147
striped set, described, 161
suspend mode, described, 161
Synchronization Manager,
    described, 161
system
  changing sound volume, 148–149
  removing programs from, 51

T

Taskbar
  described, 161
  hiding/displaying, 54
  switching between open
    applications, 54
text files, remote computer file
    transfers, 64
3D Pinball, described, 56, 62–63
thumbnails, described, 42
title bars, described, 20
ToggleKeys feature, 156
toolbar buttons
  adding to folder windows, 144–145
  restoring to default, 145
toolbars
  described, 20
  Internet Explorer customization,
    81–82
Tools⇨Add Sender to Address
    Book command, 93–94
Tools⇨Address Book command, 98
Tools⇨Options⇨Compose
    command, 96, 102
Tools⇨Options⇨Send command, 93
Tools⇨Spelling command, 95
Transfer⇨Capture Text command, 65

Transfer⇨Capture to Printer
command, 66
Transfer⇨Receive File command, 65
Transfer⇨Send File command, 64
Transfer⇨Send Text File
command, 64

U

Understanding User Profile,
described, 162
Unicode Character Map dialog box,
described, 61–62
USB (Universal Serial Bus)
printer, 106
user accounts, described, 162
username, described, 162

V

vCards, creating, 95–96
View⇨Arrange Icons command, 39
View⇨Choose Columns
command, 150
View⇨Options command, 75
View⇨Scientific command, 59
View⇨Thumbnails command, 42
View⇨Toolbars command, 144
visual system warnings, 153
volume
changing system sound, 148–149
described, 162
Volume Control, described, 71–72
volume set, described, 162

W

wallpaper
described, 69
using Web page as, 87
warnings
dialog box element, 7
visual system, 153

Web pages
adding to the Links Bar, 78
background settings, 80–81
bookmarking, 78–79
copying information from, 83
disabling graphics for faster
display, 83
folders, 153
font settings, 80–81
home page display settings, 82
offline browsing techniques,
79–80
printing, 84–85
saving to a file, 85–86
search techniques, 83–84
sending as e-mail, 86–87
shortcut creation, 83
using as desktop wallpaper, 87
viewing offline, 87
Web site certificate, described, 161
Web view, Enable Web content in
folders option, 153
windows
button types, 21
Control-menu commands, 17
menus, 18–19
opening folders in separate,
154–155
screen elements, 16–21
scroll bars, 19
shortcut menus, 19–20
title bars, 20
toolbars, 20
Windows 2000 Professional
accessories, 56–76
automatic startup settings, 53–54
shutting down properly, 14–15
startup methods, 16
Windows Classic Folders option, 153
Windows Explorer
copying a file to a floppy disk,
26–27
file sorting, 39–40
file type associations, 24
file/folder deletion, 30–31

folder creation/naming, 29–30
graphic file thumbnail viewing, 42
launching an application when
  opening a file, 36
moving files/folders, 34–35
network drive/folder permissions,
  134–136
opening, 144
renaming files/folders, 24–25
screen elements, 42–43
shortcut creation, 46
viewing file lists, 41–42
viewing file properties, 40–41
word wrap, WordPad text wrap
  settings, 75
WordPad
  bullet point insertion, 75
  date/time insertion, 74
  described, 56, 72–76
  document creation, 73
  document previewing, 75–76
  font settings, 75
  opening an existing document,
    73–74
  saving changes to a document, 73
  search techniques, 74
  starting, 73
  text selection/deletion
    techniques, 74
  text wrap settings, 75
  undoing last action, 74
workgroup, described, 162
workstation, described, 162

Notes

Discover *Dummies*™ Online!

The *Dummies* Web Site is your fun and friendly online resource for the latest information about *...For Dummies*® books on all your favorite topics. From cars to computers, wine to Windows, and investing to the Internet, we've got a shelf full of *...For Dummies* books waiting for you!

Ten Fun and Useful Things You Can Do at www.dummies.com

1. Register this book and win!
2. Find and buy the *...For Dummies* books you want online.
3. Get ten great *Dummies Tips*™ every week.
4. Chat with your favorite *...For Dummies* authors.
5. Subscribe free to *The Dummies Dispatch*™ newsletter.
6. Enter our sweepstakes and win cool stuff.
7. Send a free cartoon postcard to a friend.
8. Download free software.
9. Sample a book before you buy.
10. Talk to us. Make comments, ask questions, and get answers!

Jump online to these ten fun and useful things at
http://www.dummies.com/10useful

For other technology titles from IDG Books Worldwide, go to
www.idgbooks.com

Not online yet? It's easy to get started with *The Internet For Dummies*,® 6th Edition, or *Dummies 101*®: *The Internet For Windows*® *98*, available at local retailers everywhere.

Find other *...For Dummies* books on these topics:

Business • Careers • Databases • Food & Beverages • Games • Gardening • Graphics
Hardware • Health & Fitness • Internet and the World Wide Web • Networking • Office Suites
Operating Systems • Personal Finance • Pets • Programming • Recreation • Sports
Spreadsheets • Teacher Resources • Test Prep • Word Processing

IDG BOOKS WORLDWIDE
BOOK REGISTRATION

We want to hear from you!

Visit **http://my2cents.dummies.com** to register this book and tell us how you liked it!

- ✔ Get entered in our monthly prize giveaway.

- ✔ Give us feedback about this book — tell us what you like best, what you like least, or maybe what you'd like to ask the author and us to change!

- ✔ Let us know any other *...For Dummies*® topics that interest you.

Your feedback helps us determine what books to publish, tells us what coverage to add as we revise our books, and lets us know whether we're meeting your needs as a *...For Dummies* reader. You're our most valuable resource, and what you have to say is important to us!

Not on the Web yet? It's easy to get started with *Dummies 101*®: *The Internet For Windows*® *98* or *The Internet For Dummies*®, 6th Edition, at local retailers everywhere.

Or let us know what you think by sending us a letter at the following address:

...For Dummies Book Registration
Dummies Press
7260 Shadeland Station, Suite 100
Indianapolis, IN 46256-3917
Fax 317-596-5498

BESTSELLING
BOOK SERIES